CALLED TO ACTION

Fran Beckett comes from a single-parent family background and so knows from first-hand experience something of the joys and heartaches that that can bring. She entered local authority social work at an unusually early age, in her teens, which coincided with her becoming a committed Christian. What convinced her about the relevance of Christianity was the consistent love and acceptance of a Christian family nearby.

Since then she has been involved in student counselling and evangelism, and church-based pastoral and community work. She is currently active in a ministry of enabling Christians within the Shaftesbury Society, and across the denominations, to demonstrate the reality of God's love through caring action in their local communities. This includes teaching, training and encouraging church leaders and others; consultancy work with churches; and co-ordinating a training scheme for inner-city church workers.

CALLED
TO ACTION

Fran Beckett

Foreword by Clive Calver

Collins
FOUNT PAPERBACKS

First published in Great Britain by
Fount Paperbacks, London in 1989

Copyright © Fran Beckett 1989

Printed and bound in Great Britain by
William Collins Sons & Co. Ltd, Glasgow

Contents

FOREWORD

Quietly and almost imperceptibly winds of change have been blowing through the evangelical churches of the UK. The result has not resembled the devastation of England's infamous hurricane of 1987 but there has been a distinct change in the ecclesiastical landscape.

Some have spoken of a "sell-out" to the social gospel. Others have despaired of a glib and naive triumphalism which affirms that all we need do is "speak the word", and our country's woes will be resolved.

In the background local churches and fellowships have perceived the hurts and needs of others within the community – the elderly, handicapped, homeless, disadvantaged, unemployed, depressed and many more. Often we know the theory of how to take them the message of Christ's love but sense the incongruity of doing so without also addressing their personal needs.

The result has been a growing determination to respond to the hurting and needy people around us. Perhaps the first indication of this lay in the growth of protest against perceived moral compromise in society. Then emerged individual caring initiatives. These have been followed by local church initiatives in prayer for social needs. This indicates a growing recognition of the magnitude of the challenge confronting evangelical churches at the close of the twentieth century.

Such action has not served as a retreat from sharing the gospel. The message of new birth in Christ Jesus, resulting from repentance of an old lifestyle and commitment of the future to Him, lies at the heart of a growing evangelical social awareness. But, it is recognized that such a gospel needs to be "lived" as well as "spoken". Like many other Christians, I made my commitment to Christ as a result of "seeing" the gospel lived as well as "hearing" it spoken. This emphasis is emerging with growing clarity in the Church today.

A friend recently spoke to me about the need to make a "prophetic statement" about AIDS. He and his wife have ended up, once a week, clearing excreta from the sheets of AIDS victims. Not surprisingly interest has been shown in their Christian message. Such is the nature of true prophetic statements!

Similar acts of care and compassion are becoming increasingly common. So is the cry from within churches and fellowships – "We can see the need, but what can we do?"

Fran Beckett writes from experience in both advising and working with local churches in seeking to serve the community. Always practical, down to earth and sensible, this book is tailored to the questions and needs of individual churches and fellowships.

Rarely have I read a book which so blatantly scratches where churches are openly itching. Fran's honest style takes the reader systematically from non-individual concern to direct participation in community life. By skilfully weaving real-life stories into the text, she maintains a high level of sympathetic interest. I found it hard to put the book down and even the appendices were packed with information and ideas for action.

If you wanted just another challenge to see the hurts

in our world, this is not the book to read! But if you, and the church to which you belong, feel that "God has called you to action", then read, learn and digest the pages which follow!

I have known Fran and watched her in action over the past few years. She has always had my profound respect. I am therefore delighted to be able to add this word of congratulations for what I believe to be far and away the most helpful new book I have read this year. But, be careful who reads it – people will consider these pages and not fail to discover within them the meaning of the title – that each of us is "Called to Action".

CLIVE CALVER

14 November 1988

PROLOGUE

◆

A Dream

Imagine you are in the middle of a very vivid dream and you are taking part in something like a police identity parade. You are seated in a room on one side of a two-way mirror. On the other side stands a line of assorted people. They can't see you but they are aware of your scrutiny and they are self-conscious in their mannerisms and facial expressions.

It's a line of seven very different people. The first person seems to be some sort of business executive. He is dressed in an immaculate dark suit, with a copy of the Financial Times under his arm and a briefcase in his hand. Next to him is a harassed looking young woman with a crying baby in her arms and a toddler clinging to her skirt.

As your gaze moves along the line you see a student in faded jeans and sweat-shirt, and then an older darker-skinned woman dressed in a sari with open-toed sandals on her feet. Next to her, standing with some difficulty, is an elderly man who has the appearance of a stroke victim, with his left arm hanging limply at his side and twisted features. Helping to prop him up is a stockily-built middle-aged man with plaster dust in his hair, paint on his overalls, and what looks like a hand-rolled cigarette in his mouth. At the end of the line, and in some ways disassociated from the others, there lounges a black youth with a bored expression on his face.

13

The experience of being in such a line, and being at the end of it, is obviously not new to him.

Now to your task. A choice has to be made and in your dream you are the only one there to make it. No crime has been committed and there is no culprit to identify. The people that stand before you all have needs.

Behind the confident gaze of the business executive lies a marriage that is expiring from lack of attention. The young woman in the line struggles on her own with no partner, inadequate housing and mounting debt. The student has to sleep on a friend's floor because of the local shortage of rented accommodation and the paucity of his grant. For the Asian woman who has left behind the teeming intimacy of Bangladesh, life in our cold climate and unfriendly society is bewildering. Things are made worse for her by the language barrier and her inability to communicate with neighbours. The humiliation of dependency on others haunts the elderly man; facing the reality of it makes him retreat into depression. Meanwhile, in the pocket of the labourer is his redundancy notice and the knowledge that getting another job at his age is a futile hope. The black teenager is second generation British, yet is regularly asked what country he comes from, and told by some in no uncertain terms to get back to where he belongs. For him that creates conflict – Where does he belong? Where do his roots lie? You have to choose which person you will reach out to and help step out of that line, which one you will invite home with you that night. You know that you have no alternative but to make a choice. Whichever individual it is to be will involve you in immense personal cost. The time of decision has arrived.

Quite interesting but totally unrealistic? It is unrealistic as it stands and as an illustration has certain limitations. The people described here are in a sense stereotypes, and yet their very presence in this account forces us to consider the challenge of who they are and what they represent. For behind them are row upon row of human beings with needs, life pressures, and positive contributions to make to the world we live in. They are not lined up in neat rows; they are untidy, hurting, complex and yet possess a peculiar beauty that is a faint reflection of their Creator. They are the people who go to make up the communities in which we, as Christians, live and work and worship. When faced with this bewildering array of humanity and needs the question that presses in upon us is, "How should we respond?" In this book we will look at some aspects of life at the end of the twentieth century, how people are affected, and a range of various responses by Christians. We will try to catch a glimpse of the depth of God's feelings about the individuals who go to make up what are known as our "local communities".

This book is for people who care about the world we live in, or those who feel they don't care enough but want to do something about it. We all have a part to play, a contribution to make, some capacity to express care for our fellow human beings. Specialist knowledge or training is not essential. Particular expertise has its place but what is needed more than anything is the willingness to reach out to others with open arms.

I have written out of the deep conviction that God passionately loves people and therefore calls Christians to action. Christians from all denominations and types of churches are called. None of us are excluded. Don't pass over this book if you have no involvement in a church or don't profess to be a believer. The monopoly on caring does not lie exclusively within the Church. Christians have a unique contribution to make but we also have much to learn from others. Whatever your starting point, if you want to be a person who makes a difference then this book is for you.

You will find that the focus is mainly upon urban situations, although the principles and suggestions contained here will have a wider and more flexible application. There are many practical suggestions for action but it is not meant to be a book of instant formulas or neatly-packaged solutions. Questions are raised which could cause us to feel uncomfortable. May that very discomfort drive and draw us into the heart of God so that our response to the world immediately around overflows from a deepening intimacy with Him. My prayer is that God will in some way use this book to envision you, the reader, with hope, heavenly enthusiasm tempered with sensitivity, and a burning zeal to reach out with His love to others.

PART I

Call to Action

I

Communities in Crisis

It is essential to start with listening and observing just like it was in the police identity parade in the Prologue dream. To do this we need to look at some common features of life today and how these can affect individuals. The reason is that the person who listens is the one who can make a difference in society. Listening before acting helps ensure a more sensitive response to people. If we really want to help others we would do well to listen with all our faculties to the messages sounding out from the world around us. They can be heard through our physical environment, the media, conversations and life encounters with others, and as we listen to the turmoil that can be within our own spirits. These all have something to say to us and as we pray about what we hear, a foundation is laid for a response that is relevant because it is shaped by God.

The major cities and problems associated with inner urban communities have been prominent on the political agenda for some time now. Churches too have been focussing on the potential and challenge of urban mission, considering the validity and place of social action within this. Some of what has been said can be applied to other parts of the country. Within inner urban communities are a concentration of issues that are not necessarily unique to those areas. Life in the suburbs, outer housing estates and smaller towns has its own joys and heartaches as well. Therefore, whilst the focus here will be upon city problems the application is much wider.

If you were to play one of those association games when someone says a word to you and you have to respond by listing what comes into your mind, what would you say to the word "city"? It's difficult to pin it down to just one or two phrases because any major world city is a place of enormous contrasts and variety of images.

London, for instance, conjures up impressions of majestic historical buildings and beautiful green parks. There's a whole world of pleasure and recreation centred on theatres, concert halls, galleries, museums, night clubs and restaurants. It's a place of big business and fantastic wealth, symbolised by the bustle of the Stock Exchange and international banks. It somehow has an air of solid self-satisfaction about it – a sense of history and permanence.

Other large historical cities are similar and that is the image of the city that many have, especially those who don't live in inner urban areas. One such person is a young man called Gareth, born and brought up in the green belt area, now commuting daily into the city to work. His understanding is that it is a place from which to make money and into which he can venture occasionally to sample its delights. He doesn't see himself as having any responsibility for the quality of life experienced by those trapped there by circumstances beyond their control. His mother, on the other hand, sees the city as a place to be feared and avoided despite the cultural attractions. She reads the stories in the press describing incidents of mugging and rape, is horrified by the rising crime figures, and so her perception is entirely negative.

Both Gareth and his mother are to a certain extent correct in their perceptions. London is an enormously wealthy place and there are some who share the benefits of that. It is not always a very safe place. One family I know living in the inner city have within a year had their home broken into twice by different gangs of youths. They broke down the front door while the house was occupied, rushed in and grabbed anything valuable, counting on the element of surprise in order to get away with it. The sense of violation and fear that follows such an experience is difficult to fully comprehend. In a separate incident their teenage daughter was mugged in broad daylight. There are many such stories that don't hit the headlines because they are too common to be newsworthy. Statistics abound but it is predicted that over a four year period there will be a 50 per cent increase in crime in this country. Whatever the statistics tell us, the emotional and physical toll upon people is sobering.

However, these things only form part of our backcloth. In the city there is also a rich diversity of cultures. This is reflected in the teeming local markets where people of different colours and mother-tongues jostle each other in the business of going about their everyday lives. Go to such a market and you'll find your senses assaulted and yet strangely attracted by the profusion of different smelling spices and exotic food, the brilliant colours of bales of material or ready-made saris, the cries of the vendors pressing you to buy their wares, and the abundant variety of peoples of many cultures mingling with one another. Walk down some of the main shopping streets and you will rub shoulders with people from so many different backgrounds, including a generous portion of tourists, that you will begin to feel like a small ingredient in an enormous cosmopolitan casserole!

Move away from the main shopping streets and the crowds and you may find another face of the city where there is not so much colour and vitality. Here, the streets can be grey and dirty, with many of the shops boarded up with torn out of date bill stickers hanging off the windows. The houses have a melancholy discarded air about them; many are in a state of disrepair. Tower blocks of flats loom over you, cutting out the sun, with their entrance ways and stairs stinking of urine. Graffiti on the walls tell of the alienation and frustration of those who are trapped within an urban ghetto which they feel powerless to change.

Some of the blocks of flats have waiting lists of tenants wanting to move out but with declining availability of alternative housing the list just gets longer. In the blocks the lift may often be out of order. A pensioner such as Alfred, who has a weak heart and lives on the fourth floor, has to toil up the stairs after his weekly expedition to collect his pension. Besides all the stairs that he has to negotiate, he never knows what lies in wait for him around the next corner. There may not be anyone there, but it is the not knowing that at times becomes intolerable to bear.

Or there's the young mum, Debbie, living on the floor above him. Her flat is damp from condensation and overcrowded with the three young children who have nowhere to play. She's been waiting for a transfer for two years but because she has actually got somewhere to live she's not considered to be very high priority. Debbie feels trapped and helpless, at times desperate. The G.P. gives her tranquillisers, knowing that they will only alleviate some of the symptoms of a much deeper problem. Meanwhile, the everyday reality of life has to be faced. That includes trying to deal with an at times elusive and faceless bureaucracy who make decisions about her income, her home and her children without once asking her opinion. Picture Debbie standing in a phone box holding a decreasing pile of small change as she waits for the official on the other end of the phone to track down her papers – which have yet again been temporarily mislaid. The delay probably isn't due to callousness on the part of that individual official. It's just an expression of the "system" that seems so remote and uncaring – it provokes anger which is followed by despair and finally by apathy. Alfred and Debbie's problems have a lot to do with their environment. Blocks of flats, such as theirs, can be dehumanising but at least they provide a degree of shelter. Homelessness, however, is reaching crisis proportions in some areas and there is little hope on the horizon for those with no roof over their head.

It is estimated that there are something in the region of 50,000 single homeless people in this country. Half of them are under eighteen years of age. Local authorities have no statutory responsibility for them other than giving advice, so they end up in squats, hostels, staying with friends, or out on the streets. The Homeless Persons Act obliges local authorities to accommodate families who couldn't avoid losing their home and those who are particularly at risk. Since 1970 the number of homeless households accepted by local authorities in London has increased by 700 per cent. By 1985 the number of homeless families in bed and breakfast accommodation doubled.[1] Whole families, and particularly children living in these conditions, are often in an acute state of stress. Homelessness and poverty are responsible not only for untold misery, but for thousands of children being "at risk" or placed in care.[2]

Other inner city inhabitants who feel victims of the "system" are unemployed people. They can't always articulate the pain of their situation with words that are acceptable to those of us cocooned by our secure homes and jobs, but nonetheless the pain is real. Opinions vary and debates rage on furiously about how serious a problem unemployment actually is. Are current Government policies making a positive and lasting contribution or are they masking the real extent of the problem? Statistics are regularly issued concerning the numbers of unemployed people and there are always significantly higher numbers in inner city areas throughout the country. Statistics can be both presented and interpreted in different ways but whatever the real story, behind each table of figures are real flesh and blood people, living in their respective neighbourhoods and involved in a network of relationships. The devastating effect of having no employment in a society that values a person for what they do, does not only touch the individual without a job but the effect ripples out through that network of relationships like a stone being thrown in a pond.

Debbie's estranged husband is one of those statistics. He had been unemployed for nearly two years, despite repeated attempts in the early days to get permanent work. The pain of his loss of dignity and the accompanying sense of helplessness were expressed through a kind of creeping apathy that pervaded his attitudes and relationships. Occasionally he lashed out in anger, and he and Debbie became part of yet another statistic – one that shocks many Christians – that of a family where there is excessive physical violence in the home. In the end he could no longer face his own failure and inadequacy, often brought forcibly to his attention by Debbie as they argued repeatedly in the pressured confines of their overcrowded flat. One day, not long ago, he walked out after a row and Debbie hasn't heard from him since. He could be anywhere.

* * *

The pressurised life that many experience in the inner city is by no means unique. The large outer council housing estates also vividly show to the gaze of the passer-by the deprivation and the need that is characteristic of many of them. Listen to the conclusions drawn by a major church enquiry into the needs of urban areas: "Our visits to the inner and outer areas of the main conurbations have convinced us that it is now the large housing estates in the inner ring or on the fringes of the cities that present the most pressing urban problems."

They go on to describe what they found as they visited these estates, listened to those who work, live and minister in them, and read the various reports and statistical information. "Huge impersonal housing estates, many postwar, can be found in all our cities. They are spoken of as being 'monochrome' – that is drab, dreary, depressing, with no vitality, colour or beauty. Many outer estates are nothing less than the architect-designed, system-built slums of our postwar era. They suffer from poor design, defects in construction, poor upkeep of public areas, no 'defensible space', with packs of dogs roaming around, filth in the stairwells, one or two shuttered shops, and main shopping centres a 20 minute expensive bus journey away. Bored, out of work young people turn to vandalism, drugs and crime. The estate takes the brunt and the spiral of decline is given a further twist."[3]

A gloomy picture, with residents experiencing multiple deprivation and having little hope of being able to obtain a council transfer to somewhere better. In contrast, other suburbs have an air of complacent well-nourished respectability. Problems do exist but are kept behind firmly closed front doors. Stress and loneliness are common. Stigma accompanies the need for help because inability to cope is judged as failure. There are pressing needs here too but they are less obvious, less stark, and often less accessible.

The city has a complex, always changing, life of its own. People on the move contrasting with those powerless to change their circumstances. Whole population groupings shifting, sometimes imperceptibly, from one neighbourhood to another. A rich diversity of cultures. Cities have received, although not always welcomed, people from many other races and nations. Some are here out of choice; they are studying, or want particular work experience. Others have fled here from oppressive regimes. Yet others have come hoping to find a better way of life. Each person has brought their own culture, world view, expectations and aspirations with them. And each one is now a member of our society with a role to play and a contribution to make.

Responses to foreign newcomers have varied. There are some city areas where they are bitterly resented by locals. Hatred overspills into acts of vandalism and mindless violence against individuals and families. Vicious slogans daubed on walls express the threat that many feel from those who dress and speak differently, whose skin is darker in colour. The incidence of muggings with a clearly-identified racial motive show an alarming increase, whilst Asian children in some schools are victimised by other children. In some traditionally white working class areas of the city the threat of incomers can be very keenly felt. In one such area, where people own their terraced houses but have been hard hit by the economic recession and the closure of vital local sources of employment, certain racist agreements have been made. House owners in several roads have promised each other that if they sell their homes it won't be to anyone with a darker skin. That way the area will be kept predominantly white.

This rejection of others from overseas is not merely a recent phenomenon. We saw it in the 1950s and 1960s when significant numbers came here from the West Indies. A sad indictment upon British Christians is our failure to welcome into our midst the many sisters and brothers in Christ that were among those who came, let alone those who had no church affiliations. There grew out of that lack of welcome the formation of vibrant, supportive and culturally relevant black-led churches that are continuing to thrive and grow in the inner city today. For example, membership of the New Testament Church of God in England doubled between 1966 and 1970 from ten to twenty thousand and it is estimated that there are now well over 100,000 people in different denominational black-led congregations.[4] These churches provided a warm sense of belonging and identity, and scope for involvement that communicated worth to all who participated. This was in stark contrast to the cold aloofness experienced from British Christians. Despite the tragedy of the often enforced separateness of black-led churches they should be recognised as a positive force for good in urban areas and as an example to many of the white churches.

On our journey through the city we can't go far without encountering another group of incomers – the "yuppies" (young and upwardly mobile professional incomers) or "dinkys" (double income, no kids yet). Along with the influx of these young professionals have come spiralling house prices and large increases in rent costs in an already sadly depleted private rented sector. Many of the incomers would claim that their arrival has contributed to the social makeup of their area. An example of this is in Battersea in southwest London. As you cross Battersea Bridge you will see silhouetted on the skyline several tower blocks of flats. Up until recently they were renowned for their long lists of council tenants wanting to transfer away from them because of their poor state of repair. These same flats have since been redeveloped and are now sold to people who will readily pay luxury apartment prices for them. The whole face of the area is gradually altering with a resultant growing divide between rich and poor.

The commitment of incomers to a locality can vary immensely. For some there is no involvement because their home is seen as just being a potentially good financial investment, to be quickly discarded when there is something more attractive on the horizon. Others bring with them a greater degree of commitment. This is reflected in concerns such as wanting to see an improvement of local services like refuse collection or health care. Whilst helpful, at the same time this very process can accentuate the divide between the articulate incomer and those who feel powerless to influence anybody.

The rapid change in the social makeup of an area, often known as "gentrification", is contributing to the drain of more able local people away from the inner city. Those with middle-class dreams, or just a desire for something better, have grabbed at opportunities to move out. In other words, anyone with any "get up and go" about them has usually got up and gone! Those who have had the choice and stayed are unusual. Others have had no option but to leave because they cannot afford to live any longer in the neighbourhood in which they were raised. That means that the majority left behind are the powerless and the vulnerable, those who face crippling life circumstances but have few resources with which to respond.

It should be noted that all this has happened as much within the church as in other sectors of inner city life. In terms of the church a phrase known as "redemption and lift" applies. Christian conversion is accompanied by an improvement in living standards and Christians lose contact with the social class into which they themselves were born.[5] This in turn has contributed to the ongoing struggle of white inner city churches to identify mature local leadership.

There are certain features of city life that need to be highlighted if we are to be in any sense equipped to build bridges of God's love in action into our local communities. The city is a place of amazing diversity. Therefore, our response in Christian care and outreach needs not only to be flexible but to have a creative approach that is finely tuned to the nuances of the particular neighbourhood and to the "still small voice of God". We must avoid superficial generalisations about the communities in which we live and worship. Instead, we need to identify the previously unreached groups. They include locally born people who are unused to, and alienated by traditional church culture, language and forms of worship. There are the new ethnic groups that are changing the face of most major world cities. Besides those, there are the diverse subcultures of commerce, industry, the night, the deviant, the derelict, the alcoholic and many more.[6]

There is a growing divide between the powerful and powerless. Power is the freedom to make choices about one's life – where to live, what job to do, whether to eat at home or in a restaurant, what school one's children can attend, whether to buy a new winter coat or not – and being able to implement those choices without experiencing crippling personal hardship. There is a divide between the relatively affluent South of England and the economically hard-hit North. But there is an ever-widening gap between the "haves" and "have nots" throughout the country. It is in the inner cities and the bleak outer estates that we encounter more of those who feel and are powerless. Of what relevance and in what way should we be sharing the Gospel of Christ with such as these? This book will help to provide an answer.

* * *

There are indeed some signs of hope. Out of the deprivation are growing tiny shoots of new life nurtured by God's grace, and in places watered by the Holy Spirit through the direct activity of the church. An example of this is the recovery of the vital role of art in the inner city. Various initiatives, both secular and Christian in origin, are being set up. Some are established by self-help groups, other by voluntary organisations or churches. Through them, people are being enabled to become more in touch with their innate creativity, expressing their disappointments and aspirations through paint, sculpture, clay and other mediums. Live music and theatre declare the heartbeat of the city and its peoples. And the pain of those with no voice in society is poignantly expressed through poetry that is often raw in its intensity.

Another feature of city life is the sense of community and cohesion that spring up in the most unexpected places. Many traditional local communities were torn apart by the vigorous slum clearance programmes earlier this century. Networks of kinship, friendship among the generations and among neighbours were disrupted as people were moved out of the slums. The very structure of the sprawling new suburban overspill estates or high-rise blocks of flats inhibited contact between neighbours. However, in certain inner city areas people are still rooted in their locality. Many will not have ventured outside of a mile radius from their homes. There is a parochialism that is hard for the more socially mobile to comprehend. Church leaders often find difficulty in encouraging their congregations to become involved more in borough- and city-wide Christian events. But this narrowness of perspective can also be a

31

source of considerable strength, the quality of community solidarity being one example. Some of the ethnic minority groupings too have a bonding together that builds a strong sense of community. The priority of family life and need for mutual support in the face of a society that is often cold and rejecting in its attitude contribute to this sense of identification with one another.

* * *

So, the picture of what is happening in society and the church in the city is not totally bleak. As we saw earlier, many of the black-led churches are growing. There are encouraging moves through umbrella organisations such as the West Indian Evangelical Alliance to bring about reconciliation between black and white Christians. Other cultural congregations are springing up; their members include African, Chinese, Tamil, or Spanish-speaking peoples. Alongside these are the increasing numbers of community and house churches with an emphasis upon lively worship and shared lives. Different church groupings are rediscovering a concern for church planting, creating small new locally based congregational centres.

Again, some of the inner city boroughs, which Christians may feel they have just cause to criticise for their promotion of extreme policies, have something to teach the church. They have recognised that human beings have a fundamental need for laughter and celebration – a need that becomes even greater as poverty, deprivation, and apathy press in. Mother Teresa of Calcutta, on a recent visit to this country, talked of the poverty of spirit that she saw in the eyes of the poor she met here, something that she attributed to their sense of worthlessness. It is this poverty of spirit that has in some small measure been acknowledged, and through fun fairs, festivals, street parties and carnivals, local councils are attempting to bring joy into people's lives. These point us towards the statement that people's "chief end is to glorify God and enjoy Him for ever".[7]

In the New Testament there are various Greek words for joy – these occur a total of 326 times.[8] An experience of joy that goes beyond enjoyable events, important though they are, to enjoyment of God is essential to humankind. Some churches in recent years have begun to rediscover this vital component in their corporate life through making room for Holy Spirit inspired celebration. We would do well to listen to this because in our desire to be practical in expressing God's love we can become rather dour and earnest; problem-centred, we forget that the Kingdom of God is also about joy and celebration.

The quality of life in urban areas has been briefly but starkly portrayed in this chapter. Vivid and disturbing images from a major church report, *Faith in the City*, have been brought to our attention. Such insights may be completely new to us and alien to our experience. Whatever the level of our understanding we need to ask God to give us fresh comprehension of what it means to those who live in such conditions. The scales of prejudice have to be removed from our eyes so that we can see clearly, hearing from God what our responses should be. Maybe it will have to be an active, demanding involvement, or maybe it will be informed and prayerful concern from a distance. Whatever we understand our calling to be, we have a God-given mandate to live out the love of God in the place of His choosing, wherever that may be – in this country or overseas, in the inner city or the suburbs, a seaside town or rural community. And wherever we are, we can have that dynamic cutting edge that comes with a life-transforming love and gospel.

2

Individuals in Need

Stress! Anxiety! Pressure! A quiet desperation mirrored in the faces of commuters packed sardine-like into trains and buses. Such intimate closeness – the mingling of breath, the touch of bodies pressed against each other – and yet the aloneness, the withdrawing from contact, the muttered apologies when toes are crushed or shins are bruised. Consciousness of boredom to be faced, deadlines to be fulfilled, other people's expectations to be met. Each person locked into his or her own agenda for that day. To receive a smile or enter into spontaneous conversation with a stranger would be remarkable enough to be treated with suspicion. Isolation within a crowd.

Stress! Anxiety! Pressure! This time it is another long day alone to be faced. Battling with a body that ceases to be able to do all that its owner wants to do. Inside, wanting to run for buses, carry heavy loads, climb a step-ladder, hop, jump and skip. And the reality of frailty to be lived with.

Stress! Anxiety! Pressure! Another day of constant demands to be met. Young voices clamouring for attention, tears to be wiped away, nappies to be changed, entertainment to be provided, and confrontation to be avoided. A day when simple tasks can't be completed or are continually interrupted by the immediacy of the needs of the young. Hungry for adult conversation, yet

35

when the long-awaited opportunity arrives little to talk about except the children.

* * *

Particular features of life in contemporary Western society are putting increasing strain on the fabric of humanity. Integral to this is the disease called sin that alienates us from God, our fellow beings, and ourselves. We see it at work in individual lives and woven into the structures of society that cause people to be treated as less than "made in the image of God". The encroachment of evil, seeking to undermine what is healthy and good, can be seen ever more starkly in recent times. As Christians committed to seeing the powerful love of God being a positive force for good and turning people back to Him, we need to open our eyes to understand what is happening. Identifying the trends will help us to know where and how to respond.

As human beings we all have fundamental needs and when those needs are denied us, pressure and stress begin to build up. We have needs that are to do with our physical well-being and survival – food, drink, shelter, warmth, clothing. Sensory deprivation can have devastating effects too. Touch is important and linked with our sense of identity, with the capacity to enjoy giving and receiving it varying from person to person. Emotional needs include knowing that we are loved, accepted and valued by others. Relationships that enable us to both know and be known on a more intimate level are fundamental to our humanity. That inbuilt drive for closeness and intimacy indicate that we are made in the image of God. The opportunity to be creative and exercise responsibility, and to grow in capacity in these areas are needs that are often forgotten. Affirmation is essential for our emotional nourishment. With it goes a sense of being safe and so a freedom to take risks in new areas of life. A generous portion of laughter added to these other ingredients will contribute to the thriving of an individual.

However, there is more to us than just the physical and emotional dimensions. Alongside these and intricately linked with them is the need of every person to be restored to relationship with their Creator. Absence of that relationship leads to distortion and blemishing of all areas of life. There was a maxim that made an impression upon me as a child which has taken many years to unlearn – "you are nobody until you've proved yourself somebody". That particular understanding of human worth permeates society. The emphasis is upon being successful, getting on, coming out on top. People are valued for what they do and not for just being the individuals that they are. Meet someone for the first time and inevitably you will be asked what you do. Your reply will ensure that you are pigeon-holed or categorised in some way. We all do it. Listen to yourself when you're next in an unfamiliar social setting. Dignity is not accorded to people because of their innate worth as human beings but for the work they do, the size of income they have, where they live, and the type of car they own!

This is all relatively easy to live with when one fits the commonly agreed criteria of what constitutes a "somebody". But what happens when we don't fit that image? What of the man in his mid-fifties who feels full of vigour and capable of many years more employment, yet is called into his boss's office and told that he must take early retirement? All his adult life has been focussed on achievement at work. His identity and his work life have up until that point in time been inseparable. But now they are painfully forced apart – and what does he have left? The bottom has fallen out of his world. And yet he will have to find an answer for those who ask in the same breath what his name is and what he does for a living.

What about the black teenager who leaves school with aspirations to find a job and get on? Others have told her that it'll be difficult but she doesn't believe them. She lives in a region of the country where unemployment levels are high and she's black – which doesn't help! Eighteen months later she still has no job and now she agrees with those who predicted a gloomy future for her. Disillusionment has replaced optimism. And what value is she to place upon herself in a society that measures worth by success, and by colour?

* * *

At the turn of the century the word "family" conjured up an image of a group of people related to one another and living close together. It was not uncommon to have three or four generations under one roof, with a range of aunties and cousins living nearby. With that came support in times of crisis and social contact that created its own warmth and stability. There were exceptions and some knew loneliness. But family support was there for many, spilling over into the local community, strengthening ties of neighbourliness and contributing to a greater sense of community cohesion.

For a range of historical, economic and social reasons,

we now have what is known as the "nuclear family". This is a much smaller unit made up of husband and wife and an average of two children. The pressure to be successful in life has helped bring about a greater willingness to move where there is lucrative employment, despite the responsibilities of family ties. This increased social and economic mobility has contributed to the breakdown of the extended family. It is no longer common to have close relatives living nearby and providing friendship and support in times of need. The exceptions to this tend to be found within more rural communities or within families from other ethnic backgrounds. However, there are also signs of erosion of these values there, for example in the growing numbers of families with West Indian roots who no longer have the same once-close family ties. In many instances the nuclear family has proved incapable of sustaining itself without the support and nourishment that comes from wider kinship and friendship relationships. The divorce rate in England and Wales has increased sixfold in the last twenty years and, if present trends continue, one marriage in three can be expected to end in divorce. This has led to there being currently well over one million one-parent families in Britain caring for approximately 1.7 million children.[1]

At the other end of the scale those particularly affected by the increased social mobility are the already disadvantaged elderly. There are over one million old people in this country who have no regular visitors except perhaps for the milkman.[2] Children tend to move away from the areas in which they were brought up. They don't just move once but several times and so reduce the opportunity for elderly parents to join in their children's network of relationships. They see the support from their own generation dwindle through illness and death. Often the gap between them and their children can seem insurmountable as they live totally separate lives with no overlap save the statutary annual visit! Isolation of older people is frighteningly common. And the way in which they are valued plays a key part in this. In some cultures, elderly people are respected and treasured for their life experience, from which much can be learned. They are seen as important members of the family and the community and so are treated as such. Not so in our contemporary society. To be old is to be useless. To be old is to be seen as a drain on scarce resources. Of course there are exceptions, but that certainly is the perception of many senior citizens themselves. At the most, if you are old you must be treated kindly, your basic needs should be catered for but you are not expected to have much of a valid contribution to make. Sadly, this attitude is sometimes reflected in the life of local churches where evangelism amongst elderly people is low on the scale of priorities, and their growth in committed discipleship is seldom expected or encouraged.

* * *

Within the Church the importance of family is being rediscovered. The threat to the nuclear family is recognised; the Biblical principle of life together is emphasised. However this has often been at the expense of considering the place of the extended family, the needs of the elderly and of the single person or single parent. We need to recapture a broad view of the family, recognising the potential of the church community as an extended family in itself. This has particular relevance in a society where a sense of "family" is being lost and the numbers of those who feel alone are increasing.

Social mobility has also had an effect on general community life. A higher turnover of people moving in and out of districts has affected the contribution that people make and their level of involvement in a given area. Neighbour relationships built up over generations are now rare. A sense of community is not now necessarily related to living in a particular geographical area but may have more to do with shared interests or activities. An example of this can be seen in the local church fellowship that has a busy programme of activities that fully absorb the time and energy of its members. The result is little real contact with others in the locality who are not involved in the church. Generally, local districts tend to be less personal whilst far-off places are more accessible through easy travel and the television screen in one's own front room. The late twentieth century is witnessing a change in community as we once knew it with far-reaching implications for individuals and for the life and mission of the Church.

* * *

Alongside this, shifting attitudes towards moral standards have also had an effect. Superficiality and a lack of community commitment are heightened by a growing emphasis upon the individual. A 1987 Gallup Poll commissioned by Granada Television's "World in Action" programme, investigating the state of the nation, revealed a picture of a selfish society made up of despondent and apathetic individuals! Eighty per cent of respondents believed that the cardinal rule in society today is "everyone for themselves". Not surprisingly perhaps, seventy-five per cent accordingly viewed their children's future as "dismal" or "frightening". A climate of thought that has at its heart that sort of selfishness brings with it the attitude that if something feels good, then do it; the response to a situation that has no reference to any external guideline of what is right or wrong.

Over the years there has been a steady erosion of absolute standards – clearly agreed understandings of what is true and how those truths affect human behaviour. This can be seen in a variety of ways. For instance, the discarding of God's truth that applies to people's relationships with each other has had far reaching consequences. The number of legal abortions carried out in England and Wales in 1986 by Regional Health Authorities was 147,619. On top of this were 24,667 terminations of pregnancies of non-residents of England and Wales. It was thought by many that an increase in the number of abortions would reduce the number of live illegitimate births. On the contrary, the Family Law Reform Bill received Royal Assent on the 15th May 1987. Essentially, this Act reformed the law on illegitimacy as a recognition of the 120,000 children born outside of marriage each year.

Changing trends in personal morality are both reflected and influenced by the media. We are constantly bombarded with images of casual sexual relationships entered into for the pleasure of the moment. A well-known local radio presenter consistently engages in sexually suggestive dialogue with the listeners who phone in with comments or record requests. His conversation is certainly sexist and often bordering on racist in content. However, his show goes on and there is no sign of his popularity waning. Television soap operas, often compulsive viewing because of the absorbing nature of the complex social relationships portrayed, have certain perceptions of violence, sexuality, money and power interwoven with the plots. We scarcely notice them, but they play a part in moulding our attitudes and reactions, and particularly those of the very young.

But the erosion of moral absolutes is not confined to sexual behaviour. It goes beyond that. The use and abuse of power; the value that we put on a fellow human being; the role of money and material goods; the uses and portrayal of violence – all these things have always been with us but they are an essential part of the fabric of contemporary society that we ignore to our cost. If we are to move into a position whereby God's love and grace can become more tangible to those around us, then growth in insight concerning significant influences in society is very important, as is positive action in response.

Therefore, a question that we should address is – how are people coping with the pressure that these things help create? For it has to be lived with. Stress is now a common word in the vocabulary of Christians and non-Christians alike. Stress is a feature of late twentieth-century life in Britain and people employ different mechanisms to deal with it. Some cope by turning to leisure and recreation activities. Various forms of sport are growing in popularity but we are still largely a spectator rather than participating nation. Leisure pursuits often require money, so are not for those deprived of jobs or homes, or trapped in the inner city. Some however don't cope as well, with mental or physi-

43

cal illness as the end product. It is estimated that one in every seven people (three times as many women as men) will at some time in their lives experience severe depression. Depression is now recognised as one of the major health concerns of this age.

Escape from stress can take many guises, whether it is through retreat into fantasy or depression, the pursuit of pleasure or use of means of blunting the pain. We now spend more money in this country on alcohol than we do on clothes.[3] In the early 1960s there were 753 known heroin addicts. Specialists estimate that there are now well over 60,000.[4] This is just another form of escape from stress, albeit a tragically destructive one.

Continued pressure, and the feeling of being trapped in the circumstances that cause it, leads to frustration and anger quickly follows. Some turn that anger on themselves – depression often has its roots in repressed anger. Others lash out with unpredictable outbursts at those closest to them, causing further strain on fragile family relationships. Physical violence can become an outlet; the growth in incidents of crowd violence at football matches, for instance, is an indication of the stress in our society. Violent crime is on the increase, and the number of youths in inner city streets carrying knives has escalated rapidly in recent times. The numbers of reported rapes and occurrences of sexual abuse are spiralling. And real flesh and blood people lie behind each statistic.

* * *

There are many tragic victims of the ways of life which wrongdoing and stress have led us into. Tina is one of these victims. She has never known consistent affection or love. She doesn't know who her father is because her mother isn't sure. Her hair and skin colouring tell her that he must have been black because her mother certainly isn't. Most of her childhood was spent moving from one foster home to another. Her desperate attempts to discover how far the limits of her foster parents' acceptance extended made sure she always overstepped those limits. Rejection was a common experience. As a teenager she felt she had nothing of her own. She wanted someone to give her love. But the brief moments of intimacy were always elusive. She welcomed the rough fumblings of the men whom she allowed access to her body in the hope each time that it would be different. It never was. Hurt and angry she'd resolve that this time would be the last. It never was.

Gwen was also a victim. She was a widow in her late sixties, estranged from her only daughter who lived at the other end of the country. Gwen felt purposeless and useless. Her life had revolved around her husband. He had never shown much appreciation of her many attempts to win his approval. And then he had gone and let her down badly by dying just after his retirement. The days always seemed dull and grey. A nagging headache was her constant companion. The one neighbour, a committed Christian, who persisted in showing friendly concern somehow never managed to penetrate the wall of depression surrounding Gwen. In desperation, Gwen went one day to a church and asked them to pray about her head pains. As they prayed the pain subsided and Gwen went home with a measure of relief. The next day the pains were back. Gwen then made an irrevocable decision. Her dead body was found two days later.

But are there no stories with happy endings? There *are* tales to tell of those who have moved from a position of personal pain and brokenness to an experience of life that although not trouble-free, has a quality of growing wholeness about it that is enviable. People like Brian who spent many years in the shadowy world of drugs and violent crime, using others, irrespective of the cost to them, in order to feed his drug dependency. Or Ted, an older man embittered by the pain and frustration of physical disability. Both of them now unrecognisable because of the generosity and joy that characterises their personalities. Both now are active and caring members of local churches. And then there's Gail. Repeatedly sexually abused as a child by her father, then raped as a teenager by a trusted boyfriend, and left with a legacy of self-loathing that often threatened to overwhelm her. She is now a different woman. Fragile moments are encountered but she has a growing sense of worth and value as a treasured child of God. This spills over into an effective counselling ministry amongst those similarly damaged by abuse and exploitation. And God's heart is to see multitudes upon multitudes of broken people experiencing that sort of wholeness and abundant life.

Stress can damage people but it can also provoke us to question our values and life expectations. When materialism, employment hopes, success and relationships begin to crumble there is little left if life has been built on these foundations. As they are pursued all the more vigorously they can continue to slip like sand through our fingers, always evading our grasp.

A time for re-evaluation comes to many and a longing for something more permanent and more reliable can begin to surface – a desire to be in touch with something of a more eternal nature. A hunger for experience beyond the limits of oneself is evidenced – for those who feel rootless there is a longing to recover their roots. Spiritual hunger is on the increase. This hunger for experience, for reality, gives us within the Church an unparalleled opportunity to both demonstrate and proclaim the Kingdom of God in all its power, beauty and yet gentleness. Oh, that we would recognise what we have and want to share it!

3

Salt and Light

Individuals under pressure; fragile relationships; and fragmented communities. Yet, the Church has something gloriously effective to bring into these situations – the love of God in all its splendour and awesome simplicity. And we all have a part to play in this. Each Christian has a unique contribution to make. We have within our grasp the resources of heaven, waiting to be harnessed and then released to the benefit of those around us. The need is enormous but the potential is much much greater.

Meanwhile, what is actually happening in the Church? What is being done in response to the needs that press in on every side, clamouring for attention? Those outside the Church see it as largely irrelevant to the stresses of everyday life, and therefore wouldn't think of turning there for help. It is seldom the first place that people go to for assistance. Churches are the buildings that the vast proportion of people in our land walk past without really seeing. At the same time, there's a general feeling amongst the public that more ought to be done, that the Church somehow should be more actively involved alongside those in need.

Some do still see the Church as a source of succour. Those who are older are more likely to get in touch with a minister for assistance, but it is usually on the basis of previous contact. But there are others discovering vi-

brant groups of Christians who are remarkable for their
depth of concern. Not all churches are perceived as irrelevant or uncaring. Church is about people rather
than buildings; people functioning as a community of
believers with a shared and growing love for Jesus
Christ at the heart of their relationships; people united
in the common goal of worship that spills over into all
areas of life; people committed to telling and demonstrating the good news of the gospel; people hungry for
the dynamic power of the Holy Spirit that transforms
the principles of the Kingdom of God into reality; and
people who have the breadth of vision to see beyond
their own needs and agendas to embrace the world on
their doorstep.

The package that we call "Church" carries a lot more
with it than just a building and a group of Christian believers. And it's the total package that has fundamentally affected whether local churches have a relevant
contribution to make to their surrounding community.
Within that package we have the theological framework
that influences how we perceive society and what our
contribution to it should be. We have the layers upon
layers of experiences, both good and bad, that are woven
into the structures and life of individual churches. Over
the years, patterns of thinking and practice have evolved
that we assume are Biblical; when examined, they often
have more to do with cultural expectations or
prejudices. The location of churches and the nature of
the communities in which they're situated also affect
responses to need. And there's the people. Each with
our own set of presuppositions, particular life experience, and general view of the world. All different
shapes, sizes and backgrounds! Active or passive, com-

mitted or nominal in allegiance to Christ, and varying
shades in between. Then we must never forget the spiritual forces dedicated to undermining any work of God
through His people. They have been active down
through the generations in diverting Christian energies
into maintenance of structures, internal power struggles
and selfish preoccupations. Far more important than
our structures or ideas is the cleansing, invigorating
wind of the Holy Spirit blowing through the Church,
drawing us deeper into the heart of God and from there
propelling us out into the world.

* * *

Throughout this country there are committed Christians meeting together on a regular basis within church
buildings and houses; the people around them ignorant
of their corporate existence. They may engage in occasional evangelistic forays into the surrounding community but at the conclusion of these they withdraw
back into the safety of "normal" church activities. In
so doing, they remind one of knights of old retreating
to their castle after a brief skirmish with the enemy,
pulling up the drawbridge behind them to leave no access to the castle. Relationships with those outside the
church are either shunned or seen as a low priority.
Little space or opportunity is given for fleshing out the
gospel because life is kept very busy maintaining existing church activites. Meanwhile, outside the church
doors people are struggling with personal pain and sin,
needing to know the transforming love of God. Other
churches may not be quite so focussed on these preoccupations yet seem largely oblivious to the world around
them. Why is it? What causes this social blindness?

William Temple described the Church as the "only co-operative society that exists for the benefit of non-members". For some, complacency or apathy obscures this truth – what's more important is how we are. Many of us have an individual pietistic view of Christianity and what matters to us is our own relationship with Jesus. Consequently, church becomes something for our own spiritual nourishment and well-being, leaving no room in our lives for the untidiness of the needs of others. Maybe for others of us, our faith is such a personal and private affair that it doesn't extend beyond the boundaries of attendance at church services.

These attitudes have been bolstered by a previous widespread caution within the churches about direct involvement in social concern issues. Earlier this century, an emphasis upon the "social gospel" grew in momentum, stressing the priority of Christian's involvement in the world, bringing in the Kingdom of God in the flow of human history. This led to such a focusing upon social justice that it tended to push aside evangelism and minimise its importance. The reaction in some quarters to this emphasis was so extreme that any form of Christian social concern was seen as compromising the gospel. There was a general retreat back into the church with a stress upon separation from the world and non-involvement for fear of contamination. This doctrinal understanding is still held by those today who regard the soul as all important with the physical, emotional and environmental condition of a person as irrelevant. That early reaction against the social gospel was both understandable and right, but like many reactions the pendulum swung too far. And whilst many retreated into their defensive ghetto-like positions it was left to others, who perhaps held evangelism as a low priority, to get on with the task of responding to the needs in society. This they did with varying degrees of effectiveness.

The pendulum is now swinging back. There is a burgeoning of interest and concern to relate the gospel to the whole person. Opening our eyes and hearts to society's pain can however be an overwhelming experience. Some are afraid to peep from behind their fingers for fear of being swamped by what lies before them. Others have looked and what they have seen has caused them to back away rather than advance into the thick of it. Whilst it is only too easy to criticise the failure to press through into building genuine bridges of care into the community, it has to be recognised that churches can have inadequate resources with which to respond to the task. At least some have made moves in the right direction. In later chapters we'll look at some ways in which churches can practically respond without being swamped by people's needs or raising expectations that they subsequently can't fulfil.

Thankfully, on the whole the mainstream churches are moving determinedly away from the ghetto mentality. The reason for being in that position in the first place has been because our inward-looking agendas have had priority. As we have seen, they include a preoccupation with church maintenance, complacency, and a concern for individual spiritual nourishment that has left no room for others. Recent church history has also made its contribution with an often justified suspicion of the social gospel. The outside world has often seemed too big to tackle, too overwhelming to contemplate, and this has led to a fortress-holding attitude on the part of many church leaders. There is still a long way to go in the move to be outward looking but there are encouraging signs. Without a doubt, the Spirit of God is speaking to the Church right across the nation causing us to re-examine our priorities and open our eyes to the surrounding world.

* * *

Loving action is called for and many over the years have responded to that call. Individuals and groups of Christians have got alongside those in need. Not all, by any means, could be said to have lost sight of the reasons for their activity. Nor could they justly be labelled as the sort of people who got hot under the collar but did nothing practical. They have been in the front line of caring, ministering and working for the good of those in need, often with little acknowledgement or reward. And for us too the task has to be got on with now instead of trampling underfoot the good from the past. It is important to learn from the past and, where possible, build upon it.

Several years ago I spent some time visiting a few church-based and secular independent Advice Centres. These varied considerably in size and range of expertise but each one sought to assist local people to negotiate the "system". This involved providing information and help in filling in forms, obtaining full entitlement of State allowances, and generally understanding something of the complex world of welfare benefits. Other areas of concern included advice on housing matters, consumer law, immigration issues and provision of debt counselling. In addition to this, some were equipped to offer counselling to individuals and families experiencing relationship pressures. Not all the Centres were, or are, able to offer a wide range of expertise but many included at least one of these concerns. There were others which focussed on specific needs not mentioned here.

My task was to establish an Advice Centre at the church where I worked and worshipped. At that time there were very few church-based models that I could learn from. However, there was one that left a lasting impression upon me. A strategically situated advice agency in church premises on a busy inner-city high street. It was easily accessible to the public which was reflected in the bustle of activity inside. The efficiency and commitment of the workers to their clients impressed me. Its history saddened me. Originally set up and run by people who had a desire to express the overflow of God's love in their lives, it now held no claim to being Christian. There was no link between the Advice Centre and the church. None of the staff held any allegiance to Jesus Christ. What they were doing was valuable but over the years the motive for action had changed. The distinctiveness of the Centre, with its original Christian cutting edge, had been eroded and it had become the same as any other of this type of agency. A process of *assimilation* had taken place.

The risk of assimilation, of being absorbed into the system and losing distinctiveness, is a real one. And it needs to be faced up to by churches contemplating moving into the Christian social concern arena. It's this very fear that has caused some to hang back and not get involved at all. Others, in contrast, have proceeded gaily down this road without considering the implications of their actions. That's why very careful and thoughtful preparation about the aims, focus and boundaries of any church-based caring project need to be gone into during the planning stage. Opportunities for regular review also need to be built in along the way.

There are a growing number of groups within the Church who do have very clear concerns and objectives. There is currently a groundswell counterattacking certain evils in society. The agenda is an important one that focuses upon issues of what could be called personal morality, including homosexuality, pornography and abortion. Organisations like Care Campaigns and the National Council for Christian Standards are in the forefront of that movement. We are beginning to realise that these things are not merely a matter of personal morality but can undermine the whole fabric of our corporate humanity. Therefore, involvement in the needs of society for an increasing number of Christians means supporting these various lobbying movements. This is very important but it's not enough. *Moral indignation without compassionate action* is at best inadequate and at worst a travesty of the gospel. Care Campaigns through their work with Care Trust underline this. It is a painstaking process to find Christian families who will support unmarried mothers through their pregnancies, but through doing this they are offering a practical caring alternative to abortion as well as campaigning about it as a social evil. The horror of AIDS needs to be met not just with protests about the teaching of young people that homosexuality is a normal lifestyle option, but with sensitive and effective caring responses to those who have contracted the virus. Some Christian ministries in this field are already under way but much more needs to be done.

Recent investigations by a Christian organisation[1] attempted to uncover any church-based initiatives that had been set up in response to adult victims of domestic and sexual violence. Isolated individuals have been active in care, often with scant support from their churches, but the general picture across the country is one of woefully little being done. Yet the issue figures prominently in the media, and statistics tell us that the number of women being assaulted is on the increase. Moral indignation is not enough. Action is called for.

The slow gentle befriending of Bangladeshi families in Tower Hamlets by a young woman working with a Shaftesbury Society urban Christian Centre demonstrates something very positive. Her willingness to proceed at their pace with the relationships, to receive gladly what they offer her, and to respond practically to their need to learn English, has spoken volumes about the love of Christ in ways that are tangible to them. And in so doing she has gone some way to counteract the prejudice and racism that they have encountered since coming to Britain. Moral indignation about racism is not enough. Loving action is called for.

Paternalism is a criticism that is often levelled at earlier Christian carers – the well-meaning provision of help in times of need that seldom consulted the recipients about what they actually wanted and tended to impose solutions upon them. Both governments and churches have been guilty of this and have run the real risk of undermining the dignity and worth of the very people they sought to aid. The issue of control lies behind most paternalistic attitudes. And that for many churches is sensitive and quite tricky. Retaining control is tied up with a desire to avoid compromising Biblical standards, and not wanting to lose sight of the undergirding aim of expressing the love of God. We must be careful not to judge too harshly those from the past who have sacrificially given themselves to the needs of others, whilst recognising that they, like us, have operated within the limits of their understanding. However, the principle of taking time to consult and listen to those in need is an important one. Giving people the space to make choices and exercise responsibility is crucial and communicates something of how much they are valued as people rather than as objects of our compassion. It is not always easy to do this and at the same time hold on to those things we consider essential but it is important that we try.

Consider Elsie. She's in her late seventies and finds living on her own an increasing struggle. Her caution about asking for help lies in the fear that her independence will be taken away. That fear has been fed by the insistence of her doctor that she daily attends a Luncheon Club in a nearby church. He threatened her with residential care unless she co-operated and attended regularly. A threat jovially communicated but none the less terrifying for Elsie. At the Club she used to eat the meals that were provided and then remain sitting passively until it was time to go home. The atmosphere was warm and cosy, the helpers friendly and caring, and those who attended didn't have to lift a finger. Everything was done for them. Very pleasant, some of us might feel. But for Elsie, this reinforced what she had already reluctantly started to accept. She had become someone who was an object of care, with very little that she in turn could give. Things for Elsie have now changed. She still needs support but there is a new vitality about her. A wind of change has swept through the Luncheon Club with the members being asked their opinions and consulted about menus, activities and issues that arise. At first it was all very strange and some grumbled about the new regime! But Elsie now knows that she can give something to others. This has stimulated new confidence – including being open about her fears and hopes, and provocatively questioning the Luncheon Club workers about their beliefs.

Reading this account of Elsie's experience the advantages of moving to a non-paternalistic stance can be clearly seen. However, behind this lies the risk of letting some of the control of the Luncheon Club's running fall into the hands of those who may not be sympathetic to the Christian aims of the activity. You may feel that there is little risk here but far more if you applied similar principles to an Unemployment Project or Youth Club. The principle of honouring and valuing those in need who we are seeking to be alongside is a valid one. Equally so is the principle of serving others in the name of Jesus Christ with the object of bringing Him glory. It is how we implement these that is crucial. Therefore, the challenge that faces us is the moving out to those who are hurting in some way, holding these two principles in creative tension as we go.

METHODS

Assimilation, moral indignation without action, and paternalism have been mentioned so far. These emphases have demonstrable limitations and there are sev-

eral more positive approaches being put into operation
in churches across Britain. Each has behind it a particular theological framework and approach. They include various understandings of the relationship
between evangelism and social concern, the nature of
the Kingdom of God, the place of the ecumenical movement, and how far to enter into partnership with non-
Christians.

The *Salt Method* operates when committed Christians get involved in society and its need on an individual basis rather than from the position of corporate
action. Christians are encouraged to function as "salt
and light" (see Matthew 5:13-16) wherever we are. This
involves taking opportunities at work, at home and
through our leisure activities to release the goodness of
God into other people's lives. Awareness of the re-
straints laid upon us by our jobs is important here, as
is a desire to act with integrity. However, sensitivity to
others and to the guiding voice of God is essential. The
aim is to see the love and goodness of God permeating
society through the lives of individual Christians, and
in so doing, see the darkness of pain and evil pushed
back.

Taking it on from there, this approach also urges us
to move into spare-time activities that don't come directly under the umbrella of the local church but which
will further this positive process and expose us at the
front line of people's need. Examples include training
and working as Citizens Advice Bureau workers or Samaritans, being volunteers with one of the range of voluntary or statutory caring agencies, working with
families or individuals, becoming bereavement counsellors or hospital visitors, taking up short-term fostering,

being a helper at a club for mentally handicapped
adults, becoming a school governor or entering local
politics. The possibilities are endless and very exciting
in their potential!

The churches that are most effective in this way are
those that are careful not to give their members a mixed
message. To encourage them to be individually involved
in serving the needs of the community is one thing but
to couple that with a busy programme of church activities in which they're expected to fully participate, is
another! Instead, different spheres of ministry are recognised and efforts are made to support those engaged
in them – for example, the inner city church that has a
regular prayer group for all those in the borough playing
an active part in local politics, irrespective of their political allegiance; the larger church that has special working groups to look at subjects like housing, education
and sexuality with the aim of enabling the participants
to develop a Christian mind on these matters; or the
home groups that deliberately create opportunities for
people to share what they're doing outside of the
church.

The *Bridge Building Method* presupposes something
of a gap that needs to be bridged between a church and
its local community. Individuals may be active but the
church itself is not involved in any corporate caring response that is recognised as relevant by those living
around it. Willingness to reach out as a group of God's
people to those oppressed and bewildered is therefore
the key to this approach.

About six years ago a North London evangelical
church, with a membership of approximately eighty
people, recognised two things that were to be signifi-

cant for their future in the surrounding neighbourhood.
First, they faced up to the fact that the church was not
representative of the community in which it was
located. It was strategically situated in a large mauso-
leum of a building on the edge of a Council housing estate. However, the majority of the membership travelled
there by car and few lived within reasonable walking
distance. Consequently, their involvement in the ongoing life of the locality was minimal and there were
few natural contacts to build upon. Second, they recognised that God's mandate to express His goodness
and righteousness in the world was not being fulfilled
by them as a community of believers. A burning desire
gripped some of them to demonstrate that there is a
God who cares passionately about people, who loves us
enough to want to enter into everyday worries and
pressures.

So they did their homework. They consulted the professionals about the needs of the area and the gaps in
provision. Public opinion was sought through house to
house questionnaires. Gradually a picture was built up
of what was needed and what could be done by the
church in the light of their own resources. Consultation, discussion, planning and prayer led to the establishing of a church-based Advice Centre. They offered
information, advice, care and counsel to the general
public. Staffed by volunteers and one paid worker from
the church, funded by the church, and based on church
premises, they sought to meet needs at times of stress
or crisis.

This was corporate Christian action in answer to an
expressed local need. They are today still bringing the
love of God into people's lives through their practical

care. This is seen in the often requested advice given on welfare benefits and housing rights, the support of marriages and families going through difficult times, arbitrating in disputes, and fulfilling an advocacy role on behalf of those unable to cope with the bureaucracy of government departments. As a team they have also done a considerable amount to bridge that original gap between their church and the area, incarnating the gospel and making the Christian faith more accessible. The team itself has been hand-picked for their ability to get alongside people, and drawn exclusively from that church. They see this as important for ensuring a common goal for their work and presenting the caring face of that particular local church to its surrounding community.

Other churches are doing similar things. A Kent-based Shaftesbury Society church has recently set up a Telephone Helpline as a creative response to local need. It's also in wry recognition of the severe limitations of their tiny church premises which are not much larger than a garage and situated in someone's back garden! An inner city church acquired a run-down pub and converted it into a much needed local facility – a launderette with an attractive refreshment area and people on hand to provide a listening ear if it's wanted. In the Midlands a group of Christians are using their church premises as a Care and Community Centre as well as a base for worship. This is in an area with few facilities so they have decided to run something themselves. These projects are run by committed Christians, usually drawn from one local church, and provide a bridge for the church into the community and vice versa.

The *Christian Alternative Method* has been with us for many years in the form of church schools, most notably Church of England and Roman Catholic schools. However, in recent years there has been a resurgence of activity in the creation of alternative basic provision. These have largely come about as a reaction to the shortcomings of State provision. Independent Christian schools that are almost exclusively for the education of children drawn from Christian homes are springing up around the country. Although still comparatively small in numbers they are on the increase. Some include in their intake a small proportion of non-church children, but this is the exception rather than the rule.

Another field of care that could perhaps fit into this category is that of medical provision. Christian medical practices, some attached to churches, are beginning to emerge. Unlike the schools, these surgeries do tend to accept their patients from the general public no matter what their religious affiliations. The basic idea is that of providing an alternative that clearly shows the values of the Kingdom of God, and in so doing expresses something of His character and concerns.

Many black-led churches are establishing caring facilities that are overtly Christian for the use of the public. However, the users are drawn almost exclusively from the black community. Not only is the alternative that is set up Christian instead of secular, but it is primarily for black people. One example of this is in a church-run all-day provision for elderly West Indians who feel unwelcome in the alien culture of the nearby white Day Centre. With many of the black churches

now involved in grass-roots projects to help disadvantaged people from similar backgrounds this approach
may increase in popularity.

The *Christian Centre Method* takes many forms but
works mainly along the lines of the community of believers being one group amongst many that uses the
church premises. They have particular responsibility
for the building and are expected as individuals to
become involved with the other user groups. These
other user groups are drawn from the outside community and most would probably not claim to be Christians.

An illustration of this can be seen in one small inner
city church that has made its premises available as a
local Christian Community Centre. Other user groups
include Alcoholics Anonymous who permit no outside
participation, self-defence classes, fee-paying nursery
provision, a Parents and Toddlers Group run by the
local parents, and a thriving Over-Fifties Club. Only
the last two groups have some Christian involvement
in them in the form of church members. Alongside
these regular activities are one-off usages such as Tenants Association meetings, as well as the ongoing
church gatherings like the Sunday services and Youth
Club. Using the building in this way is meeting clearly identified local needs. Reflecting this, the Centre
Management Committee is made up of representatives
from the main user groups. Where possible, those
sympathetic with the Christian aims and ethos of the
Centre are appointed. All activities allowed on the
premises are in some way consistent with Christian
concerns although some may be totally secular in staf-
fing and emphasis. Within this, things to do with the

life and worship of the church itself are still the responsibility of committed Christians. With this particular approach, a lot seems to hinge upon the size and commitment of the community of believers, and the level of their involvement in the total life of the Christian Centre.

Finally, the *Partnership Method* has been adopted by many churches. It is similar to the Christian Centre Method but requires greater co-operation with others. For example, several years ago an ecumenical grouping of church leaders ministering in a community with overwhelming social needs came together to see what could be done. Out of their deliberations a Christian Centre came into being, situated in a defunct central church building. Since then, that building and others that were subsequently added to the project, have been widely used by different people. These have included new ethnic churches that had nowhere to meet, Asian women's groups, a luncheon club for elderly people, youth clubs, adult literacy classes, specialist client groups run by the Social Services Department, rehabilitation classes for stroke victims, and various other activities. The project has acquired several paid staff who are mainly funded by the local authority and small Trusts. They are people who are both caring and skilled in their particular field of expertise but are not necessarily committed Christians. Many of them are drawn from the area, perhaps having been previously unemployed or actual users of the Centre facilities. The picture is one of partnership – an ecumenical partnership in order to bring the project into being and then to oversee its management; partnership between Christians and non-Christians to facilitate its smooth day-to-day running; and partnership between the church, local government and the community in identifying and tackling urgent needs.

Similar ecumenical projects dotted around the country tend to be based in urban rather than rural areas. However, another Partnership approach that is growing in popularity can be seen when groups come together to tackle particular issues – for example, small locally based Housing Associations geared towards certain sectors of the community, such as young single homeless people. These tend to be established when a problem has been identified but no one church has the expertise or resources to realistically take it up. Unemployment is another social evil that has stimulated partnership. Churches and government are co-operating together on unemployment schemes that help many but have not been immune from criticism or controversy. Para-church organisations are another example of a partnership between people and churches that seeks to plug gaps in provision. Regional and national charities geared to tackle larger-scale specific areas of concern either through lobbying and campaigning (social action) or provision of caring services (social concern) are also based on partnership.

Five different approaches, incorporating different principles for action, have been described. As you have read about them opinions may have formed in your mind about the validity and effectiveness of each one. However, before we can move on to look at how you, the reader, and your church can become active in expressing God's love in your own neighbourhood we need to turn to God Himself. For without a clear and growing vision of His concern for the world, this book and all it suggests we should do, will achieve little more than being an academic exercise.

4

God's Call

An increasing number of books are being written on the
theology of Christian social concern. Our minds should
be informed of the reasons for our responsibility towards society but our hearts also need to be gripped by
the passion of God for people. We do need a theological framework to guide involvement but that will be
hollow and empty unless we have the lifeblood of the
compassion of Jesus flowing in our veins. The love of
God has to be real to us in order for it to overflow to
others in such a way that they too grasp something of
how much they matter. The purpose of this chapter is
to bring us back to God. Unless He is at the centre of
all that we do, with actions flowing out of our relationship with Him, we might as well shut up our churches
and go and join the secular caring agency down the road.
Don't misunderstand. Those secular organisations have
an important function and Christians working within
them are crucial, but the motive for all that we do has
to come from hearts that increasingly beat in tune with
God's.

How are we to know what that heartbeat is? Su-
premely, we can learn from the life and ministry of
Jesus. We can also learn from where the history of humanity started, when God created an environment and
a people, looked upon it all and saw that it was very
good (Genesis 1.31). He had brought into being some-

thing that was awesome in its complexity and splendour. Here was something that bore the unmistakable stamp of His character. This was no casual whim, no fleeting idea to be indulged, but a purposeful series of creative actions that were to set in motion a cosmic plan that reaches down through time to us today. The world and the plan for it were not activated and then abandoned to run their course. God has been intimately involved in each stage of human history. At the heart of that involvement has been His commitment to, and valuing of, what He has made (1 Timothy 4.4). Even now, this world matters to Him and remains under His government.

And what of human beings? Described as the pinnacle of creation, made in His image, and given responsibility to look after the resources of nature. Therefore, we can, with God, celebrate the sheer wonder of people! Tragically, we so often opt to pigeon-hole people as "problems" or "inadequate" or "successful", and in so doing fail to accord them the dignity they deserve. C. S. Lewis has said, "There are no ordinary people. You have never talked to a mere mortal. Nations, cultures, arts, civilisations – these are mortal and their life is to ours as the life of a gnat. But it is immortals whom we joke with, work with, marry, snub and exploit – immortal horrors or everlasting splendours." Human beings are made in the image of God, with the capacity to think, reason, and make choices, exercising responsibility and initiative. We are able to feel deeply, express a wide range of emotions, and enter into relationships that can bring healing and fulfilment. Creativity and the ability to appreciate the rich variety of the world through the senses also single out humans as being special. We as people can enter into a love relationship with our Creator – enjoying Him, experiencing the riches of His love and goodness, and giving spontaneous love and adoration in return. However, as C. S. Lewis also pointed out, we can be "immortal horrors or everlasting splendours". Something went sadly wrong. The door was opened to sin with all its evil consequences. Perhaps the chief reason that we find it hard to celebrate the glory of humanity, as created by God, is that we are only too conscious of our shortcomings. There has been a spoiling, a marring of that image of God in us.

Alienation from ourselves, each other, the world, and our Creator, has been the devastating result. Human history bears eloquent witness to that fact – as do the lives of individuals such as Jackie who despises and fears her developing body so much that she has stopped eating. Anything that is swallowed is promptly vomited up again. When she looks in a mirror she sees mounds of flesh, someone who is fat and hideous. Others see a young woman painfully thin and frail in appearance. She's alienated from herself in a very obvious and distressing way. An essential part of the healing that Jackie needs to experience is in gaining a deep awareness that she is made in the image of God, and as such is very special. In each of us the image is distorted but we all remain infinitely precious to God, and in His heart is the desire to draw us back to Himself so that we can become whole, entering into that uniqueness of relationship with Him for which we were originally made.

This all has a lot to do with the involvement of Christians in society. Our God is concerned with the whole of mankind and human life in all its intricacy. The destiny of the world is under His control and He has a vast cosmic plan to reconcile all things to Himself (Colossians 1:20; Romans 8:21; Ephesians 1:9, 10, 20-23; 3:10). Therefore, He has a concern for society and its structures as they are in the present. People matter to Him – not just as souls to be saved, bodies that have physical and emotional needs, or social beings that relate to one another, but as individuals made up of all those different parts. Some attempt to drive a false wedge between the spiritual and the physical in the world, sometimes described as the sacred and the secular. This is outworked in those who see their task as being solely to meet the spiritual needs of others. "After all, when we come down to it, it's only the soul that matters", is the opinion of those who think in this way. However, this ignores the doctrine of creation. For many of us our priorities vividly demonstrate the fact that our thinking is similar.

A woman in need encountered a well-meaning clergyman, whose reactions reflected his priorities. She later wrote this poem and handed it to an employee of Shelter:

> I was hungry,
>> and you formed a humanities group to discuss my hunger.
>
> I was imprisoned,
>> and you crept off quietly to your chapel and prayed for my release.
>
> I was naked,
>> and in your mind you debated the morality of my appearance.
>
> I was sick,

and you knelt and thanked God for your health.
I was homeless,
and you preached to me of the spiritual shelter
of the love of God.
I was lonely,
and you left me alone to pray for me.
You seem so holy, so close to God,
but I am still very hungry – and lonely – and
cold.[1]

God cares about this world and the people in it. He loves the unlovely and unlovable. He cares that people are oppressed by sin and all its effects. So, those from whom we naturally turn away, He calls us to turn towards and embrace. His is not a slushy, naive sentimentalism but a tangible, passionate and active love. That love is the lifeblood that He wants to put in our veins for the good of a needy, hurting world. Our God is not lukewarm in responding to the world. Just as He loves His creation with a burning ardour, so He hates injustice and oppression, wherever it is and whatever shape it takes. This side of God's character is sometimes too easy to forget. It's something that can make us feel uncomfortable so we keep it at the margin of our minds. The radical nature of His zeal for justice can too easily impinge upon our lives, causing disruption and forcing a re-examination of priorities. Throughout the Bible there are references to the righteousness of God. This is embodied in the persistent cry of the prophets who unequivocally proclaimed God's demand for social justice. Shallowness and hypocrisy were condemned and God's people were exhorted to choose righteousness.

An example is recorded in Isaiah, chapter 58. The

people had been grumbling at God because He had ignored their apparently valiant efforts at humbling themselves by going through the motions of prayer and fasting. The answer they received to their complaints was devastating. It also provides us with a graphic picture of what God's priorities actually are. He soundly rebuked them for their superficiality, for their pretence of commitment to a relationship with Him:

> For day after day they seek me out; they seem eager to know my ways, as if they were a nation that does what is right and has not forsaken the commands of God. (Isaiah 58:2)

He then goes on to point out that at the same time as their ritual fasting they were engaged in active exploitation of their workers. Their dealings with each other were characterised by quarrelling and aggression. Then He says this:

> Is not this the kind of fasting I have chosen: to loose the chains of injustice and untie the cords of the yoke, to set the oppressed free and break every yoke? Is it not to share your food with the hungry and to provide the poor wanderer with shelter – when you see the naked to clothe him, and not to turn away from your own flesh and blood?. . . If you do away with the yoke of oppression, with the pointing finger and malicious talk, and if you spend yourselves on behalf of the hungry and satisfy the needs of the oppressed, then your light will rise in the darkness, and your night will become like the noonday. (Isaiah 58:6-10)

Powerful words, and interwoven with them lovely

73

promises of joy, fulfilment, and deepening of relationship with God. Here, we have a turning upside down of priorities, with genuine worship and intercession going hand-in-hand with just living.

The words spoken by prophets like Amos and Nahum are frightening in the white-hot intensity of God's anger against evil. And throughout He demonstrates a particular concern for the poor and the oppressed, the weak and the vulnerable, urging His people to defend their cause. Economic and sexual exploitation are roundly condemned. Corruption of the judicial system is not to be tolerated. Idolatry, slavery and barbaric cruelty in war all qualify for His wrath. This is no weak, insipid God but one who burns with a zeal for holiness and justice, acting powerfully on behalf of oppressed people. This aspect of His character can be seen throughout the Bible. Maybe it would be easier to consign a God of justice and wrath to the pages of the Old Testament and see that as no longer relevant to today. But we can't do so because He refuses to be confined – He is here, now. Jesus demonstrated the same holy anger when He threw the money-changers out of the Temple courtyard (John 2: 14-16). And we, as made in His image, have built into us an appreciation for justice. It's often distorted but is none the less present. Consider how one of the early phrases that a small child learns is, "It's not fair!".

If we then accept that this is part of God's character we are left with an uncomfortable reality to face. The Church, as His people, therefore has an obligation to express those concerns of His for justice and righteousness. We cannot just be warm and woolly in our loving but should have a vital cutting edge about us that tirelessly works to uncover exploitation and do something about it. Those verses in Isaiah tell us of God's heart for those who are hungry, destitute, homeless and oppressed. As His people, can we do less than share that heart concern by actively reaching out to those in need with a compassion that comes from God Himself?

*　*　*

If we want to know what God is like, and how to join in with His agenda for the world, we will find the answer in Jesus. His claims horrified the religious leaders of the day, for if they were false they were blasphemous in the extreme, and for them to be true was unthinkable. He stated things like "Anyone who has seen me has seen the Father . . . The words I say to you are not just my own. Rather, it is the Father living in me who is doing His work" (John 14:9,10). There is no question that He was claiming to be God.

Jesus is God incarnate, God embodied in human flesh. An awesome and "mind-blowing" truth! It was as if God rolled up His sleeves, meaning business, to sort out the mess that His once beautiful creation had got into. In Jesus, He stepped into human history, into the midst of the pain and sin that gripped the world. He identified with us by entering our fallen world and getting "stuck in" alongside us. He shared in our humanity, with all its frailties and pressures, being like us in every way (Hebrews 2:14, 17). He experienced tiredness (John 4:6), rejection and misunderstanding (Matthew 13:54-58), hunger and thirst (John 4:7, 8), homelessness (Matthew 7:20). Immunity from vulnerability was denied Him (Matthew 2:13-16) and yet He didn't sin (Hebrews 4:15). There were also experiences

75

of tenderness (Luke 7:37-48), of joy (Luke 10:21) and of warm friendship (John 13:23; 15:15). Here was someone who was truly human. The challenge of the incarnation is that God didn't love us from afar. His love motivated Him to come among us, to get involved, not as an untouchable angelic being but as flesh and blood, bone, sinew and muscle. A person. This was identification that was costly in the extreme. And it's what He calls us, in turn, to do: "As the Father has sent me, I am sending you" (John 2:21).

Our commission is to embody, to incarnate, Jesus in the communities where we live, work and worship. It's now over to us to roll up our sleeves and to mean business in bringing Jesus into the world.

It's possible to state our willingness to imitate Jesus in this costly identification with people but there is still the practicality of that commitment to be worked out. Again, we can learn much from Jesus Himself. It was said of Him that "He went about doing good" (Acts 10:38). That verse also states that He was anointed with the Holy Spirit and power, healing all who were under the power of Satan, because God was with Him. He went about doing good – what a telling phrase to describe a person by, and what an epitaph that would be to have put on one's gravestone! Although many things were said about Jesus, this small phrase in a sense sums up much of His ministry on earth. Everywhere He went goodness was released with tangible effect upon individual lives.

Throughout the gospels we read account after account of sick people being healed, of twisted, withered bodies being made whole, of unseeing eyes focussing for the first time on colours and shapes, and of deaf ears

76

being opened to hear the babble of wondering voices and to hear as never before their very own name being uttered. Flesh, eaten away and repugnant from skin diseases such as leprosy, received His touch and was transformed as if the person had been newly born. Cruel spasms of epilepsy that racked young bodies, frightening those who looked on, were banished at a word. Fresh life was breathed into bodies that were dead. There are so many incidents described that it's difficult to choose which to focus upon. There was no sickness or disease that could withstand His touch. And as He pressed on, bringing wholeness to people in need, opposition to Him grew. The very health and wholesomeness that He brought with Him highlighted the darkness in the lives of some.

In Mark 2:1-12 we have a very familiar story, one that lends itself readily to Sunday School pictures and drama sketches. It is the story of a paralysed man who had some very loyal friends. We're given no indication of how long he had been paralysed, whether it was from birth or not. However, his condition was serious enough to totally immobilise him. The only way he could get around was by being carried on a sort of stretcher – and lying on that, he arrived at the feet of Jesus. The route to get there had been tortuous. The crowds surrounding the house where Jesus was were so vast that there had been no way through. Undaunted, the four friends somehow got the paralysed man and his stretcher up onto the roof. They then dug through the roof, making a hole large enough to lower the stretcher down. You can imagine the hush that came over the place as this unusual mode of entry became obvious to the crowd. How would Jesus react? What would He do? Maybe the owner of the house was none too pleased but his protests would have been speedily silenced as a drama of a different nature was enacted in front of him.

Jesus was clear-thinking, seeing right through to the heart of the matter. He knew that humans are made up of body, mind and spirit, and that there is a close inter-relatedness between the three. Somehow, this particular man's sickness was tied up with the state of his spirit. He needed to have his separation from God, his sin, sorted out. Jesus also knew that to tackle that area of need first would cause controversy. Undaunted by this, He demonstrated His authority and compassion for the total person that lay before Him. He forgave his sins and healed his paralysis. And the man picked up his stretcher and walked out of the house. Picture the crowds pushing and shoving in their efforts to make an exit for him and yet at the same time gain a clear glimpse of this living and controversial miracle. The hushed atmosphere being transformed into a hubbub of voices exclaiming over the wonder of it all.

Why focus on this incident? In it we can see guidelines for our own responses to people. Here was someone in a very definite state of physical need. Jesus saw beyond the obvious and treated him as a total person, as someone who had something more than just a physical problem. This man wasn't labelled by Jesus as "disabled" and then dismissed. He was regarded as an individual of worth and significance. Jesus acted with compassion, insight and yet boldness as He risked the censure of the religious leaders that were watching. He spoke and acted powerfully. The man was made whole.

"Power evangelism" is currently the subject of some debate in the Church. In this story we have a classic demonstration of it at work. As we consider our role as Christians today in society, we need to ask ourselves – or better still, the Spirit of God – what place does the miraculous have in our incarnational mission? Mistakes have been made in the past and apparent failures witnessed but is this any reason to deny broken people the opportunity to be touched by the resurrection power of Jesus? The many positive stories of those who have experienced physical or emotional healing, along with coming to know God personally, press us to reconsider our prejudices and fears of the miraculous. As we live in our communites we need to react with Christ-like sensitivity to the hurt of the individual. But this must be intimately linked with an awareness of the dynamic, powerful love of God that can radically transform lives. And such a transformation is equally valid whether it is brought about over a period of time or by a very direct and specific encounter with Jesus, as in the case of the paralysed man.

This healing account also highlights the opposition that Jesus faced. Not everyone was enamoured with His ministry of love. To some it was a threat, and to the forces of evil it was something that had to be eliminated at all costs. We too, on occasions will come up against misunderstanding and opposition as we minister the love and justice of Jesus in society. As we challenge the exploitation, and demonstrate the worth of others there will be those who will criticise. There also will be those who will actively oppose what we're doing because it is carried out in the name of Jesus. It didn't surprise or daunt Him and therefore nor should it surprise us.

Although healing the sick was a vital part of the ministry of Jesus He engaged in many other activities. People's basic physical welfare mattered to Him, which He showed powerfully in His concern about the hunger of the crowds. On one occasion (Matthew 14:13-21), the disciples had wanted to send the whole crowd away to fend for themselves. Not a very practical suggestion when considering that meant that five thousand men, plus women and children, had to find food somewhere. So, the hungry were fed by supernatural provision. It wasn't just a scraping by but a generous portion for each person with even some food left over. We too, like the disciples, have the choice of shrugging off human need or demonstrating that same generosity of spirit. For them it wasn't easy. They had to exercise faith, and so do we, whether or not the necessary provision has to be obviously miraculous. Imagine conversing with the disciples after everyone had eaten and they'd gathered up the leftovers. That mixture of awe and excitement, and a sense of pleasure at the privilege of being involved. Their early anxieties having evaporated as all around them sat contented people. The goodness of God made real once again.

Jesus also welcomed, accepted and identified with society's outcasts. He had time for those that no-one else had time for. He engaged them in conversation, and if they had homes invited Himself to them. In so doing He showed His acceptance of them. Beggars by the roadside had opportunity for dialogue with Jesus. Normally, they were so much a part of the scenery they had ceased to be regarded as individuals. And certainly weren't looked upon as people of worth. Jesus turned those attitudes upside down by answering their prayers, sometimes reaching out and touching them as He did so. Touch is an important means of communication with another person. It can show that we care or understand. It can be a gesture of affection, or acceptance. This was particularly significant in the case of lepers that were healed. In Matthew 8:1-4 we read that Jesus "reached out His hand and touched the man". That man had leprosy – a disfiguring and distressing disease that was regarded as highly contagious. Therefore, lepers were never touched except by their fellow-sufferers. In that one act Jesus bridged an enormous gap in loving the unlovely. In Western society leprosy isn't a great problem, but there are other untouchables, people that are naturally repugnant to us because of a disease, such as AIDS, that frightens and repels us. Whatever and whoever it is, with the love of Jesus coursing through our veins we too can see people through His eyes and bridge seemingly insurmountable gaps like that.

Jesus healed people. He made them whole in body, mind and spirit. He released them from the domination of demonic powers. People were rescued and set free. He met their physical and emotional needs. He treated them, no matter what their background, as individuals of immense worth and significance. He wasn't reluctant to rebuke where that was necessary, showing up evil for what it really was and engaging in open and successful conflict with the powers of darkness. Nor was He slow to express compassion where that was needed – welcoming children, affirming women, and generally spreading a special warmth and light wherever He went.

In the Jesus of the gospels we have both an example and a resource. To just examine His life and then try to live out in the world the principles that He embodies would leave us exhausted and disappointed. Life could easily become like a continuous round of New Years, with resolutions being regularly made and then broken. He offers us far more than that. Available in Him are all the resources we need to lead Jesus-lives, to be Christians in the full sense of that name.

Whilst Jesus embodied His message He also explained it. Much time was spent teaching both the curious and the more committed. It was necessary that they begin to grasp what was happening. Near the beginning of His ministry, Jesus stood up in His home town synagogue of Nazareth and read a passage from the Prophets that would have been familiar to the listeners. It was taken from Isaiah:

> The spirit of the Lord is on me because He has anointed me to preach good news to the poor. He has sent me to proclaim freedom for the prisoners and recovery of sight to the blind, to release the oppressed, to proclaim the year of the Lord's favour.
> (Luke 4: 14-22)

This reading was immediately followed by the claim that its fulfilment stood in front of them in the person of Jesus. Here was a clear charter for the inauguration of the Kingdom of God. This and the many other similar things that Jesus said, provide us with not just an example to follow but definite reasons for action.

From this point onwards, He continued to announce the arrival of the Kingdom, the reign of God being evidenced in people's lives, as He outworked the fulfilment of Isaiah's prophecy. Something unique had happened – God had broken into human history in a way that He had never done before. With Jesus came an upheaval and shaking up of things that was unprecedented. Those who came to watch and listen could never be mere spectators. They were forced to choose whether or not to repent and receive for themselves the good news of the reign of God.

He spent time engaging people's minds, as well as their hearts, helping them understand the mysteries of the Kingdom. Underlining the words by continuing to embody the principles of that Kingdom, His consistent attitude was one of being deeply moved by human need. At a town called Nain He came across a bereaved woman, a widow going to bury her only son, and "His heart went out to her", causing Him to raise the young man from the dead and "give him back to his mother" (Luke 7: 11-17). Compassion and action were always linked.

He embodied His message as He knelt to wash the disciples' feet, showing them the lengths to which His love would go (John 13:1-17). His servant heart prompted Him to take the position of a menial slave in order to show as well as tell the disciples that a foundation principle of the Kingdom is loving service of each other. In our success-geared society, where people are valued for what they do rather than for being people, how we need to learn and put into practice that same principle. Compassion coupled with action, infused by the Holy Spirit, and undergirded by the Kingdom motive of humble service, is a powerful formula for ministry to the needs of others.

In order to have a full picture it is important to remember that a significant proportion of Jesus' teaching was devoted to God's plans for the future (e.g Matthew 24:1-25, 46). The central theme of those plans is the reconciliation of everything to Himself. It was through Jesus' crucifixion and resurrection that this reconciliation was made possible. Twentieth-century Christians are in the "overlap" stage – the Kingdom having been inaugurated and become a potentially powerful reality in our lives and in society, yet waiting for the final full bringing in of that Kingdom when Jesus returns again. Meanwhile, we've been given the privilege of bringing in more of God's reign, taking territory for Him. Incarnating the gospel so that the world can see and touch Jesus and respond to Him. What greater reason could we need to prompt us to go out into the world, into our own local communities, showing the sensitive yet powerful compassion of Jesus?

Through our knowledge of God, and out of our relationship with Him, flows the motive for a vibrant and passionate contribution to the society in which we're placed. God the Creator has reminded us that all human beings are made in His image and should be treasured as such. The God of justice and righteousness threatens to consume us with His holy zeal for those qualities to become the fabric of our common humanity. The needs of poor and underprivileged people lie close to His heart, whilst exploitation of any description warrants His wrath. Jesus Christ, God incarnate, shows us in a unique way how to live in community as whole people, and through the cross and resurrection offers us the resources to be able to do it. Through His ministry we see how we can bring God's love within people's grasp, and through His message we learn just why it's so important to do so.

* * *

We have been given a task that is breathtaking in its enormity and potential. There should be no illusions about it being an easy one, but it is exhilarating in its sheer magnitude. People can encounter the living Jesus through us, through ordinary mortals like you and me. Jesus' goodness and love can be experienced by others through the active life of communities of Christians. What an incredible fact – just let the truth of it soak into your being.

We are reminded by John Stott not to be naive in our understanding of this, for "incarnational mission, whether evangelistic or social or both, necessitates a costly identification with people in their situations".[2] But lest we are in danger of feeling that this is too much, too demanding and consequently beyond our capabilities, we should remind ourselves of the rich resources that are available to us in Jesus Christ.

As Christians, our identity and security are rooted in Him, we have a future and a hope:

> But you are a chosen people, a royal priesthood, a holy nation, a people belonging to God, that you may declare the praises of Him who called you out of darkness into His wonderful light. Once you were not a people but now you are the people of God; once you had not received mercy, but now you have received mercy. (1 Peter 2:9,10)

And freely available to us as we live for Him in society is:

> His incomparably great power ... That power is like the working of His mighty strength, which He exerted in Christ when He raised Him from the

dead and seated Him at His right hand in the heavenly realms far above all rule and authority, power and dominion . . ." (Ephesians 1:19-21)

Along with a new identity, security and power, we have the promise of His companionship, of His presence with us always:

And surely, I will be with you always, to the very end of the age. (Matthew 28:30)

PART II

Resources for Action

5

Know Yourself

The heartbeat of God's love for the world beats loudly and insistently, intruding upon our consciousness, challenging our complacency, and drawing us after Him. He is calling the Church to be the instrument of His compassion. It is said of Him in the Psalms:

> Righteousness and justice are the foundation of your throne; love and faithfulness go before you.
> [Psalm 89:14]

It is the reality of these words that the Church is both commissioned and empowered to express. The Church has got the job.

We're faced with a world in need, a community on our doorstep. What can we do? What difference can we make? How can our gifts help? Initially, our choices lie between responding to people's pain or not. Having made that decision, there remain further choices – which person and how to help? We are the Church, and as such it is our unique responses that ultimately count. Our attitudes, reactions, strengths and weaknesses all matter. It is as we look into the mirror of God's character and agenda for society, and begin to relate it to our own, that the choices with eternal significance attached to them are made. For it is people like you and me who have been given the task of making real today

God's love for others. An exhilarating as well as somewhat scarey thought!

Choices, such as those described above, are not made in a vacuum. Ingrained attitudes, either positive or negative, will help determine each response. Inner fears can inhibit spontaneity, whilst preoccupation with the business of day to day survival often limits concern and insight into other people's situations. There are times for all of us when we can just about keep our heads above water. For some, these experiences last longer than others. For instance, mothers with young children at home, single parent families, disabled people, those caring for adult dependents, and people engaged in busy and demanding professions. As described in earlier chapters, life in the inner city or on run-down outer urban estates holds for many its own unique pressures. So for those already under stress, and perhaps feeling near breaking point, talk of reaching out to others in need can seem insensitive. It can place unnecessary burdens of guilt upon people who are already struggling.

The question to be asked is – how far are these stressful activities themselves an expression of God's love? Are they an overflow of His life in us? Or are they occupations that we have filled our days with because somehow they seem safer than the adventure of building bridges of compassion towards others? For many it will be the former and the responsibility lies upon the rest of us to consider practical ways in which we can relieve the pressure in their lives. Limits can be imposed by our life circumstances but even within those there may be room for creative expression of the goodness of God. June exemplifies this. She is an able single woman, in her early forties, who has chosen to live at home to care for her increasingly mentally and physically frail father. The frustrations and demands of her situation are not to be minimised but somehow within them she has discovered grace. The grace to care for her father with an at times startling gentleness. And yet the grace to also spend time writing letters of encouragement to people in prison. June's situation is unique to her but it is the hard-won attitude within it that evokes admiration and respect.

However, there are many of us that remain untouched by the majesty of God's purposes or with compassion for the needs of society. We are more concerned about our own situations, our desire for fellowship, and possibly the latest gossip. There is, tragically, far too large a proportion of the Christian Church that thinks in this way. How we all need to turn and look afresh at the living God so that our vision can be renewed and small-mindedness left behind! Naivety and ignorance contribute to this. Constantly bombarding us through the television screen come pictures of war, violence and overwhelming human deprivation. With frightening ease we can become immunised to the pain that is nearer home. And deadening of sensitivity is a natural companion of naivety and ignorance. It takes various forms. For example, those who haven't experienced the powerlessness of many inner-city inhabitants find it difficult to understand their situation. Descriptions of the stress and squalor that can accompany tower-block living are met with indignant questions such as "Well, why don't they move out if it's so awful?" On the other hand, it can be less personally demanding to passively accept at face value outward signs of respectability. Suffering lying behind a neighbour's closed front door goes unnoticed and there is no point of contact with their need.

A recent interdenominational gathering of women vividly illustrates possible attitudes in response to human need. The subject of the meeting was God's concern for the world. It was a moving and challenging occasion and several remained behind afterwards. One woman wept for the pain of others, feeling powerless to do anything about it. Another, Sue, spoke of her own experience of marriage breakdown and homelessness. There was hope in her eyes as she stated her resolve to reach out beyond her problems and the need to survive them, to those going through similar circumstances. She was determined to press through her circumstances.

An older woman named Emily described bitter years of loneliness in the midst of a busy church until an encounter with God that turned her life upside down. He caused her to see for the first time the needs of others and the unique part she could fulfil in response to them. Katie sat at the back of the room crying whilst people gathered around to hug and to pray for her. The talk of other's needs had not touched her save to remind her of her own. Ruth, the group leader, shared her desire to see the local church involved in corporate caring action. The enthusiasm was obvious and yet so also was the frustration with being unable to motivate those around her. Others trickled slowly out of the meeting, chatting about how nice it was to have fellowship with each other, and completely untouched by what they had heard. Updates on what was happening in certain people's lives filled their conversation under the guise of concern rather than gossip. Some individuals left hurriedly, preoccupied with the pressure of the immediate. Their minds full of thoughts of shopping to be done, meals to be cooked, and children to be collected from school. There was no room in their lives to embrace others. That would have to come later, when there was more time.

A fairly typical group of people. Nothing unusual about them. In fact, in the range of their reactions they're probably quite like us. Maybe we should add a few others in order to have a more representative group. Perhaps someone who questioned the theological accuracy of one of the speaker's sentences and consequently failed to hear what was important. And another deafened by the fixed opinion that the Church's priority for now is to get its own house in order before taking on the needs of others. Some stuck in the ruts of prejudice, patronising attitudes or a sentimentality that doesn't engage with reality. And most important, a few individuals with a quiet determination, strengthened by what they had heard, to do something positive however insignificant it might seem.

Prejudice is a powerful force, not always easily recognisable in ourselves. It's usually easier to identify in others. For all of us, there are certain individuals or groups of people whom we naturally regard with a sneaking suspicion or outright dislike. To Bob, they are "them" while the groups he feels comfortable with are "us". For him, it is articulate middle class people with an academic background that make him feel distinctly uncomfortable. For others of us it could equally be feminists, black or white people, homosexuals, prostitutes, the local Conservative or Labour Party, or particular characteristics in an individual that trigger a strong negative response deep down inside. Reactions like these need dealing with if we are to move out in love towards others. They can be tackled by first identifying who the "them" groups are in your local community. This should be accompanied by acknowledging who the "them" people are for you. Then bring those insights to God in repentance, asking Him to replace the negativity with a release of His love.

One way of coping with prejudice or fear is by being patronising. Lack of appreciation of the grace of God towards us individually gives rise to patronising others. The feeling of somehow being superior, being more together as a person, that spills over into how we talk about and to other people. Like those of us whose sarcastic humour is always quick to highlight the weakness of others. Reducing people to labels or pigeon-holing them as problems dehumanises, and makes a mockery of the gospel. That attitude will only be counteracted as we grow in awareness of the powerful grace of God. It's the experience of that grace, and knowledge of our human frailty, that enables humility and stimulates a kind of holy awe as we look upon the wonder of another human being created in God's image.

Graham feels strongly about things. In fact, he has a tendency to be swayed by feeling rather than reason, taking up causes for a period of time and then dropping them to move onto the next one. Sometimes those causes are issues of injustice, but unfortunately they are often people. Individuals with pressing needs are adopted by Graham. He brings them home at all hours of the day or night for his wife to feed and his children to entertain. But the initial flush of warm feelings rapidly evaporates as he is faced with the messiness of their situations. He is governed by unthinking spontaneity, a *sentimentality* of attitude that fails to perceive the realities of life for others. Consequently, he often does more damage than good. Maybe he is a somewhat extreme example. However, sentimentality in any form is to be avoided. It is an attitude that is superficial in its responses, trivialising the other person's situation often to the point of undermining their intrinsic worth. It is the sort of attitude that gushes over a golden-haired little girl in a wheelchair but is later repelled by the basic necessities of changing her incontinence pads. In Jesus we see no trace of sentimentality. And we, too, should guard against it, asking God to enable us to see through His eyes people as they really are.

Well-meaning enthusiasm is closely linked with sentimentality. Unfortunately, enthusiasm of that nature can quickly lead to being sucked into things to the point of getting out of our depth. Some of us are easily stirred by a rousing call to action from the pulpit or when confronted by someone asking for assistance. We rush in "where angels fear to tread", making unrealistic offers of help or promises that we think the other person wants to hear. There is little consideration of the limits imposed by our own shortcomings or by the complexity of the situation. Realisation of the implications dawns later, as does the necessity to deal with them! It is essential that we recognise the limitations of our individual maturity and expertise. This is especially true when responding to people who have suffered disappointment or rejection from helpers in the past. The temptation to take on the role of "rescuer" can be great but it can lead to a repetition of the very experience from which we were wanting to rescue the person. Recognition of personal limits is healthy. And bringing them to God for Him to work on, creates space for growth in capacity to sensitively care for others.

Some women at that interdenominational gathering rejected what the speaker said because they were frightened of getting involved. *Fear* can be an attitude that is powerful in its effects, paralysing action and reinforcing apathy. The different fears that inhibit being alongside those who hurt are at root quite similar. The risk of being overwhelmed and unable to cope is real. Deprivation and personal pain are never tidy. They tend to spill out all over the place, often messy and resistant to being fitted into neat formulas or categories. There is a daunting unpredictability about reaching out to someone in pain. The systems and structures we encounter on behalf of others can be equally deterring in their inflexibility. And so, the potentially overwhelming nature of need within society prompts many within the Church to retreat into the safety of known pursuits. The fear of being swamped leading to passivity and seeming disinterest. However, this doesn't have to be so. It is true that it is not possible for a church or individual to embrace all those around them that need support and care. An attempt to do the impossible will only lead to failure or breakdown. Recognising that, there still will be for each of us unique opportunities. How to go about identifying these possibilities more easily is outlined in later chapters.

Let us return to Emily. She was the older woman who remained behind at the end of the interdenominational gathering. The greater part of her church life had been spent feeling unappreciated and excluded. She used to occasionally bemoan her fate to God, questioning Him as to why people paid her such little attention. She never waited long enough to hear the answer to her question. Until one day in desperation she came to Him again and this time lingered long enough to listen to the reply. All God said to Emily was – "I love you. I love you and I want you to love others too". Simple words, of the sort she had heard expounded in umpteen sermons, but somehow this time the truth of them reached right into the core of her being, effecting the beginnings of what was to be a radical reorientation of her attitudes.

Surprising herself, Emily began to take risks. Instead of waiting for others to come to her she began to tentatively take the initiative. As she prayed and worked at it, her fears and resentments subsided. They were replaced by an emerging sensitivity to the inner promptings of the Spirit, guiding her to approach various people. Mistakes have been made. On occasions old patterns of reacting have resurfaced, needing fresh dealing with. However, her new-found boldness has now extended beyond the church to her neighbours. She has discovered a new dimension in a life previously dominated by fear. And many lonely elderly folk now have an understanding and compassionate visitor in the person of Emily.

The key to getting her started was an encounter with God and a deep revelation of His love for her. From there, it has been a matter of growing in relationship with Him. As that relationship has developed, so has her capacity to grasp who God wants her to spend time with. For Emily, this has involved taking risks, making herself vulnerable to the misunderstanding or rejection of others. It hasn't always been easy but there was a vitality, a sparkle in her eyes, as she described what her life had become. Emily had moved from a position of fear to one of reaching out. Although her eyes had been opened, the scale of what she saw failed to overwhelm or paralyse her. Instead, purposeful care, with clear boundaries based on available time and ability, fill her days.

* * *

For many Christians, it's not so much the scale of need in the community as the fear of somehow being contaminated by it. To emerge out of the confines of the Church could lead to compromise with the world, an abandonment of values and principles that are held dear. That risk, too, is a genuine one. There have been casualties along the way. Individual Christians have become so identified with the agenda of others that they've lost their distinctive "cutting edge", and in some instances even lost their faith.

History should teach us wisdom, not inaction. Perhaps in our fear of compromise with the world by venturing into it, we have not recognised how the world's priorities have crept into the Church. Power, prestige and status preoccupy us, whilst buildings and traditions often matter more than people. This is a far cry from the values of the Kingdom taught and modelled by Jesus. A healthy caution is valuable and should stimulate prayerful assessment of the nature and reasons for involvement. From that basis, action can be taken. Alongside this, substantially more attention needs to be given to finding ways of supporting those Christians who are already out in the community getting on with the task. Informed care should be their experience, not niggling criticism. Listen to the words of Jesus concerning His plans for His followers:

> My prayer is not that you take them out of the world but that you protect them from the evil one. They are not of the world even as I am not of it. Sanctify them by the truth; Your word is truth. As you sent Me into the world, I have sent them into the world. [John 17: 15-18]

A sense of personal inadequacy, of being ill-equipped and inexperienced, is a fear that many have. It is helpful to recall that the nature of all unhealthy fear is to prevent positive movement. Therefore, an awareness of shortcomings that just leads to inertia comes within that category. Rather, self-knowledge should drive us into the presence of God, who can turn around our weaknesses, motivating us into meaningful activity. Recognition of lack of experience can be a prelude to change. There's a pin-on badge that is quite popular in some circles. The wording on it says, "Please be patient – God hasn't finished with me yet!" Each person has a unique starting point when they begin their relationship with God. We bring with us an equally unique package of life experiences, hurts and fears, prejudices, ambitions, talents and personality attributes. It is as that package is brought to God within a framework of commitment to co-operate with Him, that the "making whole" process can go on. Hence the wry accuracy of the wording on that badge.

Consciousness of our weakness coupled with a willingness to take risks with God, gives Him access to work in and through us in ways only previously dreamt of. Our very vulnerability can make us into people who are sensitive to the heart cries of others. We can begin to view them through God's eyes as our negative attitudes are supplanted by burning compassion. Fear is pushed back by love that is strong, tempered by wisdom and free from sentimentality. We have the potential to become people in whom can be seen something of the loveliness of Jesus. And that above all else is what this sad, sin-sick yet infinitely special world needs.

* * *

STRENGTHS AND GIFTS

Some all too readily focus upon searching out their own negative attitudes, uncovering their weaknesses and examining them from every angle. If you talk to them about having certain strengths of personality or gifts from God, they will brush these aside in their haste to remind you of their failings. At the opposite end of the spectrum are those who revel in praise and cannot bear to hear anything negative said about them, however true or necessary it might be. We all fit somewhere within or between those two extremes. The apostle Paul reminds us:

> Do not think more highly of yourself than you ought, but rather think of yourself with sober judgement, in accordance with the measure of faith God has given you. (Romans 12:3)

We must apply that principle by the Spirit of God to the negative attitudes that we entertain and then move on. It is now time to examine the other side of the coin, going through the same exercise in relation to positive individual strengths and gifts. The "sober judgment" mentioned above, coupled with faith, won't lead to an emphasis on either inadequacy or superiority of personality. Instead, it is the pathway to realism and can open the door to adventure with God in the world.

What personal strengths are necessary in order to be effective in building bridges of relationship and care into the community? Professional *expertise* can play a valuable part but more fundamental than learned skills is what we are like as people.

James is an accountant, highly successful in his job and generally respected in his local church for his obvious administrative abilities. Trevor is a hospital porter by profession. He is a member of the same church as James but stays more in the background. Obviously ill at ease in large groups, he often finds it difficult to articulate what he's thinking. The two men hold in common recent contact with a young family that had started to attend the church.

It had transpired that this family were struggling with financial and housing problems. It seemed sensible that James should use his expertise to advise them. Accordingly, he arranged an appointment for them to see him at his office in order to discuss their finances. Throughout the subsequent interview, the family hardly uttered a word. However, James swiftly and efficiently worked out a housekeeping budget. He rebuked them for spending too much on food, and then ushered them out of the office with the promise of further help should they need it. After this they continued to spasmodically attend the church but seemed to avoid James, and so, with a shrug of his shoulders, he did nothing more about them.

Meanwhile, feeling rather nervous, Trevor called in to see them at their flat. He sat playing with the children, drinking tea out of a mug, and offered to help find a better job for the husband through his contacts at the hospital. From then on, he visited regularly, often shy and hesitant in his manner but always prepared to listen and to care. He helped them gradually redecorate the flat, and after several months managed to put the husband in touch with a suitable job.

Outwardly, James had what was needed to help that family. However, his lack of *sensitivity* undermined their already fragile sense of self-worth. Imposing a budget upon them, offering criticism from the lofty position of having an income at least four times bigger than theirs, did little to help. Maybe those initial difficulties could have been overcome if he had persisted. Matters between them might have improved if he had followed them up by visiting their home, seeking to listen and to understand what life was like for them, and trying to build a relationship of trust. In contrast, Trevor had none of James' verbal skills or financial expertise. But he did have a measure of sensitivity and displayed "stickability" in his willingness to pursue involvement with them. He was the one who actually showed the love of Jesus in action.

Sensitivity to others is a strength to be both sought after and treasured. It means a growing ability to understand something of another person's situation and pain. The capacity to identify in such a way as to stand alongside, offering support when it's needed, and standing back when it's appropriate. Not superimposing upon others one's own feelings or responses from a similar situation but treating them as individuals, very special individuals. Feeling with them, but not getting so sucked in that the boundaries between what is their perception and what is the helper's become unrecognisable.

To be sensitive doesn't mean to be passive or weak. It's to do with an active reaching out to another person, trying to see the world through their eyes and hear it through their ears. Some of us are naturally quite sensitive people and therefore more easily wounded. If that is the case, a work of the Spirit of God within us is required. That sensitivity needs redirecting away from susceptibility to personal slight to being more attuned to God's voice and more tender towards others. The truly sensitive person is not weak. For them, there can be a place for confronting what is wrong but on the basis of relationship, and with the motive of love.

How willing to *serve* the needs of other people are we? Very often it is those who stay out of the limelight who are getting on with the job of serving others. They need recognition and further release into a ministry of compassion in society. Serving others can be confused with being a "door-mat" sort of person, taken advantage of and trampled upon. This distorted understanding again has more to do with passivity and weakness than Christ-like service. True service involves active consideration of the interests and needs of those with whom we come into contact. It includes treating people with dignity. It means putting ourselves out for them in such a way that their range of life-choices are extended, and not so that they become overly dependent upon us.

Underpinning it is humility, and awareness of the generous grace of God.

Trevor served that family, working with them to improve their quality of life. The way that he went about it demonstrated their worth. Their dignity was not undermined. How conscious an attitude that was we have no way of knowing. Perhaps it has a lot to do with the type of man that he is? Maybe you are not an obvious leader but you care about putting other people's interests first. The menial tasks tend to come your way, or at least the ones that don't seem very spiritual! Be encouraged. It may well be that in you God has someone that He can greatly use to make His love and compassion tangible to human beings. Whether or not it feels like it, you are a person with a unique destiny and calling. He is calling you to join with Him in the adventure of faith.

Trevor had staying power. *Perseverance*. A quality of steadfastness that caused him to return to that family again and again. Initially, it wasn't easy as barriers of suspicion had to be overcome. At times progress seemed to be painfully slow as he listened to the same stories being repeated. A relationship was being established but on occasions he wondered what on earth he was accomplishing. Questions about the value of his visits niggled away at the back of his mind. However, as time passed by gradual changes came about. Their physical surroundings improved. An air of stability crept in. Trust was built so that deeper issues could be explored and questions asked of Trevor about his faith.

We live in an instant age – instant mashed potato, microwave ovens, computers and radio waves. Turn on the tap and water gushes out. The pace of life has speeded up and instant results are expected where perhaps it's not right to do so. Relationships are not instant but are built slowly and painstakingly. Years of deprivation or long experiences of loneliness are not cancelled out in a moment.

There are occasions when God does miraculously intervene, dramatically transforming a person or a situation. We could certainly do with more of those! However, He calls us to a quality of stickability, that attitude which keeps on persevering no matter what the opposition. A steadfastness that refuses to treat people casually or superficially, that doesn't discard them if they fail to meet our criteria of respectability. That quality of heavenly stickability is needed if we are to demonstrate anything of God's loving concern for His creation.

Closely allied to perseverance are *reliability* and *consistency*. Part of our human frailty includes making rash commitments or promises that we never intend to keep, letting others down as a result. Disappointment is a common human experience. We all know at first hand how devastating it can be to be let down by someone else. A truth that God wants us to grasp is that His love is totally and eternally reliable. He is utterly consistent and not swayed by irrational whims or moods. Promises that He makes He keeps. For the ordinary person in the street that concept remains rather remote and meaningless if it is read about but not experienced. That is where the Church, and in particular individual Christians, come in. Wisdom in the nature of commitments made which leads to them being honoured, can actually make God's love more real for others. If our reliability is an overflow of the love of God in us, then others will be able to get hold of what He is like, making it easier to rest their security directly in Him.

Psychology degrees or social work qualifications do not guarantee Christ-like compassion. They provide valuable insights and training which have validity but they are not necessary for all of us. Sensitivity, a servant heart, perseverance, reliability and consistency are all important attributes if we want to join in more fully with God's agenda. They need refining and maturing so that there can be unique expression of them through our individual personalities. Growing maturity in these qualities is more important than paper qualifications and will help equip us for the task in hand. Specialist skills will be needed at times and people with them can usually be found making it unnecessary for us to get out of our depth when dealing with complex human beings and organisations.

Practical skills and spiritual gifts also play a strategic part. Identifying with others and getting involved in their lives sometimes requires getting our hands dirty. Like Jane, an inner city church worker who spent ten hours in the local Casualty Department with an injured elderly woman who had no living relatives or friends. Follow-up included cleaning and decorating her house, fixing the plumbing, feeding the six cats, and providing assistance with bathing and toileting when she was discharged from hospital.

There are those within the Church who view themselves as essentially practical people and therefore feel they have little to offer. On the contrary, it is those people who can vividly demonstrate through their actions that God cares about the everyday details of human beings' lives. The small act of changing a plug or light bulb for someone crippled with arthritis can make all the difference. Cooking a meal for a single parent with young children can provide a brief but much needed respite from everyday pressures. There are innumerable examples of creative practical care that if expressed sensitively and from a servant heart can make a tangible and significant impact.

The subject of *spiritual gifts* is vast and complex. However, a rigorous assessment of ourselves would be incomplete without asking what God has placed within us. Here, some people are confused. If we recall that God has a purpose for the world and He is inviting us to participate in that, then it makes sense that He also makes available to us the resources that we need.

God gives gifts so that we can be more effective for Him. Out of the lists of grace-gifts in Romans and I Corinthians there are several that immediately have particular relevance. The gifts of showing mercy, encouraging and serving others are fundamental to the Christian's ministry of compassion in the community. Consider the different dynamic at work when those qualities are expressed in the power of the Holy Spirit rather than out of mere well-meaning enthusiasm.

The more exposed that we become to the pain of others the more essential it is that we are tapping into God's supernatural wisdom and insight. Failing to take hold of those resources will lead to realisation of those previously mentioned fears of being swamped by needs or drawn into compromise. When faced with the complexity of another human being's entanglement in problems and sin, supernatural revelation that clarifies what is happening can be so important. That is not to deny the value of human logic or acquired counselling skills but more to remind us that they are not enough in themselves.

And what about the miraculous gift of healing? God's touch on a life that restores and renews either physically or emotionally. The subject of healing is surrounded with some controversy and debate. Mistakes have been made, and in some cases insensitive handling of situations has led to unnecessary heartache. On the other hand, the direct intervention of God, bringing healing into people's lives, does happen. Suffice it to say that Jesus' encounter with people in need often included physical healing. We must ask ourselves whether His concern and purposes for people have fundamentally altered since that time? If not, the responsibility is upon us to co-operate with Him, being prepared to venture into a climate of deepening and active faith in His healing power.

Administration is also referred to as a gift and is one that is perhaps more comfortable to consider than healing. It's something that lies more directly within our experience and can even be regarded as mundane. However, it is a gift from God, and as such is important. This can be especially so as we support those struggling to make sense of the "systems" and bureaucracy in society. For example, the need for debt counselling is on the increase. Consider how valuable the gift of administration could be, along with serving and showing mercy, when getting alongside those with financial problems.

CONCLUSION

Our focus has been upon Christians as individuals rather than upon the Church. If we have the goal of becoming more effective for God in the world, it is essential to have a growing awareness of our personal attitudes, fears and prejudices. We are the Church, and as negative qualities are individually dealt with, we will be empowered to corporately embody the warm yet powerful love of God.

Our attitudes affect the choices we make, and how we perceive ourselves is central to this. If we want to mean business about bringing the love and goodness of God into the world around us, then the time has come for a vigorous reassessment of our individual attitudes, prejudices and strengths. Not an exercise in introspection but a prayerful appraisal of who and what we are, and what by God's grace we can become. Nor should it be an exercise to make us merely feel better, although greater wholeness can be a glorious by-product. Rather, it is something that will give insight and create space within for God to change us into people who incarnate His love in a powerful way.

Looking at ourselves and how we relate to people can be a threatening experience, yet it is at the point where we are put in touch with our own frailty that new beginnings can come into being. It is also a time when we can discover strengths and gifts that are ours that have not previously been acknowledged. We will learn that we are less than we thought we were, and mysterious-

ly, infinitely more than we considered ourselves to be
as well.

The ability to listen well is implicit in all that has
been said. The necessity of giving time to really hear
what others are saying instead of foisting preconcep-
tions upon them. Listening in such a way that we give
people the room to speak about things that trouble
them. Listening to the heartbeat of society, having our
ear to the ground to recognise trends and issues at a
local as well as national level. And undergirding all our
listening, an open inner ear to the voice of God. It
means being prepared to open up the turmoil of our
thoughts to Him so that they can be calmed and clari-
fied. We then can hear more easily His affirmation of
love towards us. The still small voice of God prompt-
ing and guiding, making sense within a world of con-
flicting demands and opportunities.

Know yourself. Not endless introspection, but the
searchlight of God revealing hidden fears and attitudes
so that wholeness can be brought in. A discovery of the
wonder of being who He has made you. All the potential of His resources being made freely available to you.
Catching the vision of His glorious purposes for the
world.

And it is when all that we are is harnessed, and then
released by the Spirit of God into the world, that people
will begin to grasp in a new way that there is a God
who cares about them. The act of bringing ourselves to
God, and doing so again and again, will enlarge our capacity to both receive and express His love for others.
Then increasingly, our hearts will learn to beat in time
with His.

6

Know Your Church

The needs around us in society continue to clamour for attention. However, our personal resources should be becoming clearer to us. We're planning action within the framework of the Church, and in order to do that we need to know our own local church well.

Your church. What picture comes into your mind as you consider that phrase? A familiar building and an intimate knowledge of which seats or pews are the most comfortable? Or maybe it's a serried rank of heads with faces and bodies registering various degrees of attentiveness to the sermon? Perhaps certain individuals prominent in the ministry of the church, or time-consuming activities that make particular demands upon you come forcibly to mind?

Whatever scenes flash through your imagination, an integral part of the process of bridging the gap between church and community and involving the church in serving the local area is that of undertaking a rigorous assessment of church life. It means going beyond an easy acceptance of the familiar status quo. It means asking questions about activities and structures, the reasons behind them, and their effectiveness for the Kingdom of God.

This may seem quite far removed from community involvement. What has the internal life of our local churches got to do with concern for those around us?

Building bridges of care into the community requires resources. Each local church, whatever the size of congregation, possesses resources that can be used to make the love of God a reality for those in the vicinity. The scale and variety may vary considerably, with some feeling that they have little to draw upon. The majority of illustrations used in this book are drawn from urban settings, with the recognition that many urban churches have small memberships. Some may feel that they are literally struggling for survival and it takes all their energy to maintain existing activities, let alone have enough time to contemplate new thinking, but whether large or small the basic resources in a local church will be similar. There will be people with their gifts, practical skills and time. There may be a building, and some finance that can be utilized. A creative assessment of the resources available within our churches will contribute significantly to the process of determining the way ahead and deciding which methods to adopt.

When we build our bridge of care into the community we need to take into account that people may actually walk across it! What will they find when they reach the other side, when they venture into our churches? The quality of corporate life and mutual care within our own church should be looked at in some depth. Even though it can sometimes be a threatening and troubling exercise for some, it can equally be an extremely valuable experience with benefits that are reaped over a long period of time.

Note what proportion of the congregation are active and who are constantly in the background or passive. Why is this happening? Is it to do with your organisational structures or unwillingness to take risks in giving others responsibility? Or maybe they don't want to be too involved? If so, can anything be done to tackle what is holding them back from fuller commitment? This has nothing to do with negative, critical judgments of individuals but is about recognising the resources that we have in people, in each other, with the aim of enabling many more Christians to discover their potential in Christ. Therefore, honesty and realism, undergirded by a willingness to change where necessary, are essential ingredients for this whole task of getting to know your church.

PEOPLE RESOURCES

Our number one resource within the Church is people. Clear needs within the community may have been identified. There may be vision and enthusiasm for a particular course of action but without people, and the right people for the job, little can be accomplished. Few churches are beset with the problem of too many willing workers! A more typical picture is that of an overburdened inner core of individuals doing most of the jobs in their church. They are often more articulate, and usually have more obvious leadership abilities than others in the congregation. And when there is a fresh task to be undertaken it is to them that all eyes automatically turn.

If that is a description of the situation in your church then perhaps the time has come for a radical reappraisal of what the inner core are doing and the reasons for the inactivity of everyone else. Those of us who have responsibility for inviting others to take on jobs within the church need to examine our expectations and understanding of what constitutes a leader or a "good worker" in a particular sphere of activity. A close look should be taken at those on the sidelines. Why are they there? What are their unique gifts and skills?

Ada and Ivy had attended the same local parish church for years. Both in their mid-sixties, quiet and unassuming in manner, they had become such a familiar sight that they blended into the background. Little was expected of them except the occasional slot to be filled on the flower rota. Ada lived on her own in the house where she was born. She had never married and had worked up until her retirement as a clerical officer in the Civil Service. Meanwhile, Ivy lived with her sister and brother, and had worked in various jobs in the retail trade. Both lived within walking distance of the church and attended faithfully over the years. Whilst their faith was real to them, their public participation in church gatherings was characterised by diffidence. If the leaders thought about them they were considered much the same as each other, largely because they often sat together in church services. To be honest, little was really known about them as individuals, and no real consideration had been given to what gifts and skills they might have.

This description of Ada and Ivy's participation in their church can now be relegated to history. Things have changed for both of them. With gentle encouragement they have come to the point where today they are key members of their church's caring initiative in the community. They function as individuals, with different areas of responsibility that draw upon their unique strengths. Ada welcomes newcomers to the project, putting them at their ease, and communicates the warmth of the love of God in an uncomplicated fashion. Ivy visits people at home, befriending the lonely, and demonstrates a remarkable consistency in her quiet care. Both have grown in confidence, more readily contributing in planning and prayer for the project. Active contribution there has spilled over into the life of the wider church, and they no longer blend into the background in the same way. Nor are they overlooked any more.

An encouraging account which contains a vital principle. All members of the body of Christ, the Church, are important and each has a unique part to play. For too long we have overlooked those who don't fit our particular criteria or whose concerns don't neatly slot into the existing church structure. We need to become more creative, more adventurous in our understanding of the variety of ways in which individuals can serve. People are a vital resource to be treasured, nurtured, and released into effectiveness for the Kingdom of God!

Any consideration of people resources within a church cannot be divorced from their gifts. Emotional and spiritual maturity will influence the expression of them but the responsibility remains upon the leadership to help individuals identify what lies within. Gifts of mercy, administration, pastoring, evangelism, and others may exist in an embryonic form and need careful drawing out.

For example, take Mark and Sue. A couple in their late twenties, with a somewhat stormy marriage, generally regarded by their church leaders as not yet mature enough to take on any responsibilities. Theirs was a large church with a high proportion of motivated and able people. Consequently, Mark and Sue tended to be carried by others rather than looked to for a contribution. This did little for their self-esteem. However, the co-ordinator of the church's Care Centre for elderly people saw potential in them. She approached the leadership about inviting Mark and Sue to become part of the team in their spare time. The leadership took some convincing but her certainty won them over. She believed that between them Mark and Sue had pastoral and administrative gifts, which although raw and undeveloped could in the right context be encouraged to grow. So Mark and Sue joined the Care Centre team.

It was not all plain sailing by any means. They needed quite a lot of support and structure in their work. However, despite occasional problems, their inclusion in the team proved to be a successful experiment. The assessment of their gifts had been perceptive, and as time went by it was a delight to see them operating with fresh confidence. By inviting them to join the team, something of their worth had been communicated to them. Through using their gifts with increasing sensitivity they were enabled to grow in maturity and relationship with God. As well as this, their marriage was strengthened by the opportunity to serve together in the church, and they themselves gained enormous encouragement from seeing people in the Care Centre positively assisted.

Mark and Sue's gifts hadn't been utilized but Brian, member of another church, suffered from being misplaced. As a deacon in a Baptist Church he had responsibility for building maintenance and some administration. He fulfilled his duties reasonably competently but was sometimes troubled by the lack of enjoyment or satisfaction that he gained from doing so. Then came the opportunity to help out on a soup-run, supplying food late at night for the homeless people who slept rough in the area. The thought of it made his heart pound and caused a funny butterfly sensation in the pit of his stomach. He rebuked himself for being foolish – such activities were for the younger men in the church, and his duties as a deacon were already far too time-consuming. Thankfully, he had a far-sighted minister who on hearing of Brian's reaction encouraged him to go along on a trial basis. For the minister this was a risk because he stood to lose one of his more reliable deacons. However, he had recognised Brian's untapped gifts for some time and was committed to helping him discover a creative outlet for them.

Brian didn't look back. What had been a cautious experiment on his part became the focus of his spare time. He discovered an ease in establishing rapport with those who lived on the streets, building relationships of trust and care. Eventually, he took early retirement and devoted himself full time to the formation of a local Housing Association catering for those he'd contacted. Needless to say, he gave up his responsibilities as a deacon. In fact, he ended up drawing the church much deeper into work amongst homeless people, including setting up the Housing Association!

When considering the resources that lie within the local church practical skills should not be forgotten. These can be especially useful for practical expression of care in the community. Some churches run action-based projects that are geared towards the needs of those who are in some way more vulnerable. Their work can include decorating the homes of elderly people, doing the garden of a disabled person or teaching adolescents at risk the rudiments of car maintenance.

Jim is a man in his early fifties. A couple of years ago it seemed as if his life had come to an abrupt end. With no warning he had been made redundant from a job that he'd held for twenty-two years. All his life he'd worked with his hands and now there was nothing for him to do. The first six months were spent on every conceivable practical task in the home until there was nothing left outstanding. Despite the generous redundancy payment he became depressed and listless.

Instead of his church recognising Jim's predicament and the value of his practical skills, all they saw was a depressed man who wasn't much of a public speaker and lacked spiritual confidence. However, a friend of his from another church saw in Jim just the man that was needed to help with a new ecumenical unemployment project. It took a lot of persuasion but Jim is now happily occupied in a job that he sees as being of use in the community as well as personally rewarding. The project is geared towards those who have tried other unemployment schemes but have failed for various reasons to get permanent work. Jim teaches them basic decorating and house maintenance skills and takes small groups into the community to learn on the job. The homes they go to are ones in particular need, with referrals coming from a wide range of agencies and churches.

Various people's stories have been used to illustrate the tapping of resources within the individual local church. Many more could have been told, including some that don't have such happy endings. The vital element that often makes the difference between success and failure is that of relationship with the people concerned. Drawing upon people resources from within the church is not to be a cold and clinical exercise, conducted at a distance with little personal knowledge of the individuals concerned. It should be done on the basis of deepening relationship and understanding, taking time to listen to their concerns and interests. Room should be given for people to try new things, with the safety net of acceptance and affirmation readily available despite mistakes made along the way. In so doing, it is made more possible for the compassion of Christ to be released into a hurting world.

PHYSICAL RESOURCES

The dividing line between whether our church buildings are a valuable asset or an ever-present headache is sometimes a difficult one to draw. Many churches were built for a bygone era with little thought given to future changes in need and usage. Some externally imposing inner city churches are so delapidated on the inside it would cost a fortune to thoroughly renovate them. The majority of church buildings in this country are vastly underused. Little consideration is given to that fact and meanwhile they lie closed and uninviting. What a negative impression seedy-looking and closed up buildings can create in the local community!

One such church, built in Victorian times to seat over five hundred people, now has a congregation of forty. They have to meet under the balcony because that is the safest area in the church. To sit elsewhere would put the congregation at risk from falling plaster! However, all is not lost. A new look to the crypt area is being planned with the creation of a Family Centre and Coffee Shop included in the range of innovative possibilities.

Those fellowships, such as many of the new churches, that have no permanent building of their own have a different problem. The advantage of being without the potential millstone of premises to maintain is marred by having no base in which to hold activities, and no focal point of identification for the local community. Ways around this can be found by entering into partnership with others, taking advantage of space in their under-used churches. There is an example of this in Bethnal Green where an old Shaftesbury Society mission hall is used for youth work activities. Alongside them is a growing black-led church which has recently launched there a Care Centre for elderly people. As a result, that building resource is being almost fully utilised in a way that meets local need and is bold in its expression of God's love. Creativity and flexibility are pivotal qualities when thinking about the use of buildings. Don't be afraid to dream dreams and explore all sorts of crazy ideas! Sometimes our lack of imagination causes us to miss heaven-sent opportunities.

Of course, in all this the commodity that comes quickly to mind is that of finance. So often it is lack of money that undermines vision and causes enthusiasm to evaporate. Acknowledging financial realities does not have to lead to paralysis of action. A delicate balance between faith and financial considerations does exist.

However, the bottom line is that if a particular project is something that comes straight from the heart of God, then all the resources will be provided. Sometimes we give up too easily.

What is required of us is an informed and creative approach, rooted in prayer and kept in motion by faith. Take advice. Consult those with expertise in tracking down different sources of funding. Use the various handbooks that are available to give information about how to tackle the task. And pray.

Take a step back and consider objectively what money there could be within the church. Are there creative ways that haven't previously been explored of releasing finance? The practice of setting up extended households was adopted by some churches in the 1970s. One of the by-products of these experiments in living was that more money was made available to the church through the pooling of resources on a household and inter-household basis. Although mistakes were made during that period, perhaps it is time we learnt from them and some of us considered pursuing simpler and communal lifestyles, freeing financial resources for the work of the Kingdom? Another consideration is whether the actual project itself could be self-financing in some way. This is applicable to some unemployment and environmental projects. Also worth bearing in mind is that some types of caring projects are eligible for government funding.

We haven't yet come to the end of the list of resources within the church. Some Christians have a pattern of living reminiscent of the White Rabbit in *Alice's Adventures in Wonderland*. They rush hither and thither, from one activity to the next, only stopping to check their watches and mutter under their breath about being late. However, time is a commodity that should be included in our resource list. Shorter working weeks, job-share opportunities, unemployment and early retirement all mean that there may be people within the church who have more spare time than previously.

We saw earlier that Jim suddenly had a lot of time on his hands. Sadly, the potential of this went unnoticed by his church. Jim's feelings of failure were inadvertently reinforced and the church missed out on a valuable asset.

Sensitivity to the individual situation and a realistic approach are important when thinking about what time people might be in a position to contribute to a new community initiative. Obviously, there will be varying levels of commitment and maturity, and people's capacity for work does differ. Assumptions and prejudices tend to come to the forefront when considering resources that are related to people. Beware of placing the heavy burden of your unrealistic expectations upon others.

However, through a process of discussion, do be prepared to explore new ways in which time could be made more available. Perhaps someone in the church would be willing to babysit for two mornings a week so that a young mother could be freed to take an active role in a new initiative? What resources are there? And how could they be creatively utilised for the benefit of the local community, the good of those involved, and the glory of God?

OUR SIDE OF THE BRIDGE

Demonstrating the love and justice of God in society is a mandate that comes straight from the heart of God. As we have already seen, the expression of that can vary greatly. Whatever form it takes, questions and interest will be provoked. Whether intentionally planned or not, a church which takes this mandate seriously will build a bridge of care into the community. Bridges are also built when individual Christians show care and give reasons for their actions in a sensitive manner. The existence of these bridges will mean that people may venture across them into the local church – so the question to be asked is "What will they find on the other side?" And this is a question that, if possible, should be addressed before launching any new initiative.

The consideration of people and physical resources within a church as suggested earlier in this chapter, can be a troubling and threatening exercise unless sensitively carried out. The next step, that of conducting a radical appraisal of corporate life and the effectiveness of existing structures, can be quite daunting for some. It may be threatening for the leadership who feel responsible for the current state of affairs, and for a congregation who can feel under scrutiny. It could well be that they have invested years of their lives into particular activities which may in reality have borne little obvious fruit. Change within the church can be an unsettling prospect for people who already feel bewildered by a rapidly changing and increasingly impersonal outside world. This all needs to be recognised and therefore special attention given to using unthreatening appraisal methods. An appraisal is necessary but sensitivity in approach and timing can make the difference between ultimate success and failure.

Attitudes are not usually written into church constitutions but often have a far greater influence than those things that are there in black and white. Are the attitudes commonly held within your church conducive to making newcomers from any background feel at ease?

Ted has been in the same church for most of his sixty-five years. He grew up through Sunday School, then the teenage church organisations, and eventually joined the church as an adult. As he grew older he took on various responsibilities, always retaining a special affection for the building and all it symbolised for him. A few years ago, changes began to occur within the life of his church. No longer did all those who attended wear their Sunday-best clothes. Many of the younger men dispensed with suits and ties, replacing them with jeans and open-necked shirts. No longer was there the same need to peer around extravagant hats in order to see the preacher. Hats became a phenomenon that was largely confined to weddings. There seemed to be far less respect and reverence than there had been in the past. The sense of solemnity and occasion during the services was elusive.

Poor Ted found all this very difficult to cope with. He resented the incomers with their casual ways. Strong prejudices against lateness to meetings and what he regarded as irreverent attire emerged in regular complaints to the leadership. He couldn't understand why the format and content of services had changed, why the language used was less formal, and the times altered to accommodate people too lazy to get up on a Sunday morning! His church was being spoilt and all that he held dear trampled upon for the sake of those who came in from the outside.

The attitudes that Ted displayed are not unusual. Values rooted in a certain culture had come to mean more to him than Biblical values of hospitality, love and acceptance. He couldn't see beyond the externals to what was really important. In fact, the heart and essential purpose of that church's existence had not been lost. It was people and their relationships with the living God that mattered. Changes had been introduced that acknowledged the culture of the day. That church strove to minimise, without compromise of the fundamentals of the faith, the sense of alienation that unchurched newcomers could feel.

If our churches really do exist for the benefit of nonmembers what attitudes will greet those who venture across our bridge of care? Those who do may not all look or smell very respectable. The unlovely person may come through our doors as well as those who are instantly likeable or attractive. Will they be judged by the clothes they wear, language they use, and lack of understanding of our church culture? Or will they be greeted with an acceptance that supercedes barriers of unfamiliarity and demonstrates something of the warm love of God?

It is not merely a question of older people learning to accept the different ways of the young. Admittedly, for many that will be difficult, and it is important that each generation is valued enough to be listened to so that insight can be gained. It may well be that an older person who visits a predominantly young church is expected to "liven up" in order to fit in. Or the common situation where all newcomers are regarded through the "spectacles" of white middle-class culture, with anything that doesn't fit into that considered strange or unacceptable.

Other unhelpful attitudes include the White Rabbit syndrome of busily rushing around with important things to do. Consequently there is not enough time to greet newcomers properly or make the beginnings of relationships with them that can be subsequently followed up. This syndrome is common among church leaders! The attitude on the part of members that regard church as existing to gratify their needs means that the focus will be inward-looking, often resulting in cliquish behaviour and a desire to perpetuate their own particular ways of doing things.

In Ted's story there is an amusing postscript. Slowly, and at times painfully, his attitudes changed. Biblical teaching, the example and friendship of others, and above all the renewing work of the Holy Spirit in his life, led to growing flexibility. There were still aspects of the changes that he disliked but he no longer got all hot and bothered about them in the same way.

A situation which epitomised the transformation he'd undergone occurred one Sunday evening at church. The service was well under way when in through the door wandered a middle-aged man. He had obviously been drinking heavily. Apparently, he was also feeling hot, because all he had on were his shoes, socks and underpants. Hardly the correct attire for church! Instead of having a minor apoplectic fit on the spot, as he would have done in the past, Ted moved swiftly into action. Courteously but firmly, he steered the man out into the foyer, drawing in some help as he went. He had certainly altered in his attitudes. Incidentally, so had most of the rest of the church. There were no muted exclamations of outrage or shocked mutters from the congregation. Their capacity to cope with the unusual had grown considerably. This was just another instance of the church being confronted with a needy world.

The quality of corporate life, the relationship between members, is also significant. Many of those crossing the bridge into church will come conscious of personal need. They will be looking for something. The life experiences they bring with them may well be of heartache and rejection. In the world around they'll see people divided by race and colour, class, educational background, age and financial status. Inside the church it has to be radically different.

The local church has the potential to be a ready-made caring community, representing different groups in society but none of the divisions. Love, trust and mutual affirmation characterising relationships instead of gossip, mistrust and one-upmanship. Within the very fabric of corporate Christian relationships, despite human frailties, there is a potent force for good. A positive model of the reality of God's love can be shown to others – ourselves, with God in the midst.

What will hurting people find when they venture into the local church? A closely knit, yet generously inclusive group of individuals, who reach out in a welcome that is healing in itself? This is not idealism but attainable Biblical reality. It is something that we must strive for with all our might, taking hold of the resources of God to bring it into being. It's not an end in itself or an excuse for turning our backs on a broken world until we are ready for it. Rather, the deepening quality of corporate life becomes a priority within the wider consideration of the church's role in society.

Affirming attitudes and positive relationships will go a long way in breaking down barriers that exist for newcomers to a church. There is, however, still the cultural gap, and a need for activities geared towards those enquiring about or new to the Christian faith. If you, the reader, are a middle class Christian, the assumption that you have never played Bingo in a Bingo Hall is probably correct. Imagine what it would feel like to venture into one, on your own, for the first time. A potentially bewildering experience as you discover where to sit, what to do, and what the rules of the game are. It will take a while to interpret the terms used by the caller, with the language of Bingo being new to you. Perhaps you won't know anyone there – will someone rescue you and show you what to do?

This experience of an alien culture is akin to what is encountered by those going to church for the first time. Put yourself in their shoes. Religious language is used and people appear to understand what the different terms mean. There's a confusing array of books to choose from or spidery writing on an overhead projector screen to decipher. This is accompanied by spontaneous singing with apparently everyone but you knowing the words. Then there's a talk by an austere figure seemingly describing another planet! This may not be quite the caricature that you think. If the local church is to have relevance in its community, then attention should be paid to the cultural gap that can exist. This means looking at the language used, illustrations given, and practical application of talks and sermons.

Teaching methods need to be evaluated so that truth can be communicated in a comprehensible fashion to all those that listen.

Finally, questions need to be asked about existing activities and church structures. This is perhaps the most threatening part of the whole exercise of getting to "know your church". Many of the activities within a local church's calendar were originally established with a sense of vision and purpose. Over the years, a considerable amount of time and physical and emotional energy may have been invested in them. This can make it difficult for those involved to look at them objectively. However, without regular review they can lose their way, becoming aimless and irrelevant but kept running because they are there. Structures were never meant to become ends in themselves. Instead, they are to be tools, vehicles for the expression of the purposes of God and flexible enough to meet diverse needs and situations.

A review of existing activities should include an assessment of how effective each one is – whether they are fulfilling their particular aims, fitting into the broader goals of the church, and achieving growth in some way. Are they inclusive and geared towards responding creatively to newcomers? Depending on the scale and method of community concern pursued there may well be a need for a special series of services or an enquirers group established. This should link in with the evangelistic programme of the church. Alongside that, thought will need to be given to the means by which pastoral care and support through times of difficulty will be extended to newcomers. Can existing groups cope with this, should it remain within the domain of the caring project, or should a new structure be created?

Our church structures reflect our true priorities and therefore warrant regular review of this nature. Do they both equip and propel Christians out into the world, or instead suck them into perpetuating an endless round of meetings that effectively insulate them from society? We should never fear closing down redundant activities although obviously the way in which it is done needs to be carefully thought through. The people concerned may have invested considerable amounts of themselves into those occupations and so find letting go quite painful. A kind of bereavement can be experienced. Regular review of church groups and structures can reduce the likelihood of this occurring. However, where it does happen supportive loving relationships with those concerned can help ease the pain of transition, and so create space for unexpected new beginnings to be discovered.

CONCLUSION

The important principle of integrating a caring project as far as possible into the heart of the church, instead of tacking it onto the edge, cannot be emphasized enough. It is essential on several levels and will in the long run ensure greater effectiveness. Workers participating in a church project need informed support and prayer. Likewise, those functioning in society in particular ways as "salt and light" also need such support. Not many churches have a superabundance of people queuing up to become involved in a new activity. The faithful few are usually over-stretched. Therefore, if something new is being considered an overall assessment of what is currently happening and future implications for the church is fundamental.

Somehow resources have to be released, structures made relevant, and attitudes become more Christ-like. This will not happen unless we are prepared to face things as they are, seeking fresh vision for the way ahead. The more comfortable route is to avoid an appraisal of the type proposed in this chapter. In so doing, a God-given opportunity to enable church members to discover their area of ministry and the streamlining of activities for greater fruitfulness will be missed. Equally sobering is the thought that individuals may cross that bridge of care only to find within the church other gaps of culture and unhelpful attitudes which still need to be bridged.

Therefore within a climate of faith, an appraisal of what is going on and getting to "know your church", is important no matter what the size of congregation. Don't miss this strategic step out – you may be surprised by what you find!

7

—◦—

Know Your Community

Within the Church there is currently an encouraging emphasis upon going out into society with the love of Jesus, instead of sitting behind closed doors waiting for the public to venture in. Good intentions abound in some quarters but enthusiasm is often thwarted in its expression because of ignorance or naivety about appropriate outlets. Increasing numbers of people within local churches want to do "something" but they're not too sure how or what!

Fundamental to the wise channelling of that energy is being in touch with the heartbeat of the community, making a response to people's "felt" needs. It is relatively easy to make assumptions, based on limited understanding, that a certain course of action or caring project is just what the community needs. Out of short-sighted enthusiasm for a particular idea it is possible to fail to take into account the very people towards whom it is directed. People need to be accorded the dignity of having a say about their lives. This includes the opportunity to express personal opinions, needs and aspirations. And through our uninformed but energetic concern we run the risk of denying people that privilege, imposing our solutions where no solution has been sought.

So far, we have looked at some of the needs in the world around us and what we can draw upon in order to respond more effectively. However, to be effective we also need to be relevant. And to be relevant we need a growing understanding of the individuals and community we're seeking to serve in the name of Christ. In other words, we should do our homework before embarking on any new community care project, no matter what its intended size or focus.

Throughout this chapter the main emphasis will be upon churches who are considering corporate action rather than upon the initiative of lone individuals. Churches of all sizes and types could usefully put into practice the suggestions outlined here. They apply particularly to any local church that has not attempted within the last five years to get to grips with understanding their neighbourhood or parish. Even those with a long tradition of community care would be wise to take time to reassess what is happening around them, and so establish the continuing relevance of what they're doing.

When faced with the task of finding out what happens in our community, the immediate questions are "Who is to do the investigating?" and "how do we go about it?". The second question is answered in some detail in the next chapter. Churches that have small congregations, and few or no professional people except perhaps the minister, tend to think that they have no answer to the first question. If your church falls into that category, don't despair because there may be ways that you haven't previously considered.

You have four main options. The first is to abandon the whole idea of doing some homework, and to go ahead with whatever project or method of serving the community that you think best. The second option is to pay someone to come in and prepare a neighbourhood profile for you. Several of the larger denominations have people within their ranks who possess the necessary skills to help in this way. There are also a growing number of independent consultants who will carry out the task on a local church's behalf, usually for a negotiable fee. Alternatively, your church could take full responsibility, being imaginative in drawing the best out of people in the congregation who may feel they have little to contribute. The fourth option is to bring in someone with the necessary expertise to advise, and assist the exercise where necessary, with the bulk of the actual work being done by people within the church.

These all apply equally to larger congregations but because of having more people resources it is usually easier for them to take responsibility for part or all of the task. Where possible, it is important to involve the congregation. Besides giving them a good working knowledge of the area it will enable them to more easily identify with and support the end result. Therefore, no matter what the size of church, the third or fourth options are preferable.

What you need are some people prepared to give regular spare time over a period of between three to six months. Form a small team of three or four to take responsibility for the research. At least one member of the church leadership should be included in order to ensure that those making final decisions or endorsements of the findings have been party to the whole process. One member of the team should have administrative ability, being the sort of person who readily gives attention to small details. Another needs to be a reasonable communicator and able to ask the right questions to draw information out of others. It is also helpful to have someone who can maintain a broad vision and concept of the task, and who is able to reflect theologically on the findings.

Team members will all need a sense of commitment to what they're doing, a measure of stickability, and willingness to put aside preconceived ideas. They should avoid seeing the exercise as their exclusive property, instead taking opportunities to draw in others from the church – learning from their insights, and using their practical skills such as photography or typing. There should be clearly defined aims for the research. This, along with agreed lines of responsibility and communication between the local church leadership and team will prevent confusion or misunderstanding arising.

* * *

We live in a world of very rapid change. This should be taken into account if we are to be prepared to respond to the needs of tomorrow and not just today. It is therefore important that we try to anticipate what shape those changes are likely to take and how they may affect our particular locality. What happens on a broader scale in society does influence the local scene. International and national events can have significance for the individual woman or man in the street. The type of government in power and how long they are likely to be in leadership, the major laws that are passed, and general trends in society all have an impact sooner or later on the world on our doorstep.

Just as talking about the responsibility of the Church

to care can seem abstract and distance us from the personal implications, so can discussion of the trends and needs of society in general. The majority of the population lives in local communities and it's there that we need to begin. For most Christians, the significant contribution that they make will be in a local context, in the area where they live and worship. It is that local setting and how to begin to understand it, to which we now turn our attention.

A local community is never as simple as merely a collection of houses, and a haphazard group of people that happen to live in them. It is more than a particular geographical area that has arbitrary electoral ward boundaries drawn around it. The lines on a map seldom have much to do with the real limits of where one community ends and another begins.

An area may include several definable groupings of people who could be called communities in their own right. Consider a neighbourhood that has quite a few Greek delicatessen shops. The conclusion could be drawn that there is a small resident Greek community. However, there are also significant numbers of students living in bedsits and rented furnished flats in the area. Other local people are from a West Indian background, being part of the first generation to be born in this country. A recent influx of fairly affluent white, middle class professionals form an equally identifiable group. So in that one locality are several different groups of people. Each person in their group holds in common a certain lifestyle or culture and therefore they could be regarded as a community of people. The mixture described above is more likely to occur in an urban area but other co-existing groups based on age, type of work, religion or social class can be found in any part of the country.

Therefore, for the sake of clarification, the term "community" will be used to describe a local geographical area, recognising that there can be within that several levels and networks of relationships that span clearly identifiable "groups". Each "group" has embraced a distinctive way of life that gives them a clear identity but in order to live and function in an area will have developed the means of relating to other "groups", thus making up the wider community.

* * *

You have formed a team from your church, perhaps with an outside adviser alongside. Now, where are they going to start? What should they be trying to find out about the community? There are three main areas of research that can be very useful as a foundation for action. A sometimes sobering but none the less valuable exercise is to attempt to gain some understanding of how local people perceive your church. Second, there is the broad category of gaining general information about the current, and projected, make-up and needs of the community. Following on from that, is a focus upon particular groupings about whom your church has a special concern. Perhaps unemployed people, single parent families or those battling with depression? You will find in Appendix I a list of specific questions to help the team gain a clearer picture of your local community.

How does the community in which your church is situated perceive you? What do they think of you? It is time we took the risk of asking these questions and then faced up to the implications of the answers. It isn't that we become image conscious to the extent of being in some way dishonest about what we're putting across. Rather, that we begin to appreciate something of what it means to look at our church through the eyes of an outsider.

To attempt to do this may mean that we're on the receiving end of criticism. There will always be those who seek to condemn or find fault with the Church generally. The reasons for this vary. However, it would be a useful exercise to attempt to find out whether your church is seen as a place of welcome and care. Is it a place of refuge? Are you seen as having any relevance to local people? What sort of reputation does the church have? And do new people ever venture through the doors?

Take time to consider what image you are communicating to those outside. Then ask yourselves if that is the one you want to come across. For instance, the exterior of a church building speaks volumes but we can become so used to our own church that we no longer notice what it is like. Is it attractive and welcoming, communicating a sense of something going on? Or is it scruffy and uninviting, with out of date posters hanging off the noticeboard, and a general air of inaccessibility? How people see your church needs to be taken into consideration because it affects reactions and expectations of you as a group of Christians. Building bridges of care into individual and community life has to be done on the basis of trust. That takes time and some churches have already gone a long way down that road. For others, there are walls of suspicion and hostility to be broken down.

Secular caring agencies need to be enabled to see that you are not another bunch of crackpot amateurs who will quickly run out of steam. Instead, they have in front of them a group of people committed to identifying with the vulnerable in realistic ways that will make a difference. Locals will need to hear, through what is said and done, that they have an intrinsic value and are not just objects to whom "good must be done"! Credibility has to be earned and that will come about through showing real commitment to people, relationship building, and concern for the community as a whole.

Alongside finding out how others see you, research about the community itself has to be done. An in-depth analysis could take years and expertise beyond yours, so what general areas should the team focus on?

First, decide where your own geographical boundaries lie. You may not operate on a parish system but, none the less, decide what your catchment area is going to be. This may have to be altered later on because of the information you find out but it's necessary to have a starting point. It would also be advisable to ensure that you don't encroach upon another church's "parish" if you intend to set up a project on your own. Again, this can be sorted out later on when you have a clearer picture of what you plan to set up.

Questions should be asked about what sort of community it is. The range and distribution of different people groups is important. Perhaps yours is a diverse community with a broad mix of ages and backgrounds? Maybe it is made up predominantly of white professional folk, who are mainly first time buyers with young children or none at all. It's possible to gain some idea of commitment to a community by the grouping into which people fit. There are obvious exceptions to this but a nursing or student population tends to be largely transient, as do younger upwardly mobile families. In contrast those with older children, and elderly people, are less likely to move and therefore tend to become more involved in community life.

Are there any minority groups that although small in size have a significant impact upon the area? An example of this can be seen in Deptford, in South East London, where there is an unusually high ratio of single homeless men. There are various reasons for this, including the location of a large hostel, but it is obvious that their presence affects the local community.

Provision of certain facilities or types of housing can influence the siting of minority groups. As well as this, people tend to gather where there are others of like mind or lifestyle. There is a sense of support or safety in numbers for those who feel in some way threatened by society. Over many years, groups of people from other countries have sought a better life here, tending to cluster together for mutual support. The city has often been a place of greater anonymity and tolerance, so it's not unusual to come across there other examples of pockets of people who feel generally less acceptable in society, such as practising homosexuals.

The range of people living in an area will be influenced by the type and availability of housing. In some urban areas the housing market is shifting so radically that it's difficult to predict what a given community will be like in five years time. To illustrate, some churches in the vicinity of the huge Royal Docks redevelopment in London have tried to formulate strategies in response to changing needs. This has proved well-nigh impossible because of the unknown nature of all the changes that are to come there and how they will affect that area. Rural areas are also experiencing change. In recent years, East Anglia has gone through a housing boom stimulated by changes in public transport provision – this has radically affected that region.

The general questions that need to be asked about housing include – what sort of housing is there in the community? What proportion of council to owner-occupied property is there? What is being built, and what sort of prices for rent and purchase are being charged? Is there much property that can be rented? General state of repair, the availability of family size accommodation, and the length of council waiting lists are all significant details. Some indication of the scale of the homelessness problem should not be overlooked either. And finally, how are all these likely to alter over the next few years?

Employment opportunities in the area are worth examining. It can be harder to gain an accurate picture of the scale of unemployment in a community where there is quite a mobile population. There are obvious differences between residential and industrially or commercially based localities, and many living in the former may expect to travel miles to work. It's also worth bearing in mind that for some groups in the community it would be considered quite alien to travel more than a couple of miles from home for a job, no matter what you think they ought to do!

The next and very important question is – where are the people? Where do they go for leisure and entertainment? What are the popular meeting places? What communal facilities are there? Older and unemployed people can often be found in libraries where they go for warmth and conversation. For some middle-aged women the only outlet is the weekly trip to Bingo. Pubs or Working Men's Clubs are a haven for many men. Wine bars and popular eating places are often the haunt of young single professional people. Community Centres, Tenant's Association Halls, Sports and Leisure Centres can all draw in diverse groups of people for various activities but often with little inter-group contact. Particular coffee bars, pubs or amusement arcades can be adopted by groups of teenagers for a while, often monopolising them to the exclusion of others and then moving on. Toddler groups can be a source of much needed support for young mothers and the main focus of social contact. Launderettes and hairdressers can be quite key social centres too.

These are some of the significant meeting places in the community and it is important to know where they are. Finding out what local people feel they need in the community for a better quality of life involves going to where they are to ask them. At the same time you can also learn a lot from finding out why certain places are more important as social centres than others. To do this, the team can draw in other church members to help in two ways. One is to take, and create, informal opportunities for discussion about the community with shopkeepers, neighbours, and others. The second way is to use a carefully prepared questionnaire and interview people. A practical point to bear in mind here is that any publicity for a caring project that you subsequently set up also needs to be where people actually are.

Where do people go when they've got a problem? You need to know the sources of help that already exist in the community. How accessible and relevant is what is offered? Try and find out what is inadequate or missing – for instance, in many regions organisations like the Marriage Guidance Council and Citizens' Advice Bureau are struggling to cope with the number of referrals they're getting. Elsewhere, telephone helplines such as the Samaritans cover vast distances and therefore seem less approachable to some. Sexual violence is on the increase but many communities have no helpline or Crisis Centre.

To a greater or lesser degree there will be a network of neighbourliness and community support undergirding the work of the various caring agencies. This is a vital but sometimes elusive aspect of community life. It is possible to measure to a limited extent by the existence of co-operative efforts such as Good Neighbour Schemes. However, neighbourliness tends to usually be of a more informal nature. Attempts to assess it come down to public opinion. Nonetheless the strength and togetherness of a community is closely linked with the nature of the relationships that exist within it. How far is isolation a general experience or limited to just the few? Within people groups there may be bonds of loyalty but then those whole groups can feel marginalised and excluded from the wider community. Bangladeshi people in Tower Hamlets have strong kinship and friendship relationships within their own people but tend, often with good cause, to feel unaccepted by others living around them. These are very important questions to address, not least because your church can play a significant part in counteracting the isolation of some.

* * *

This all may seem like a lot of work, a lengthy and time-consuming exercise that is difficult to fit in with the other priorities of church life. However, to carry it out will prove invaluable for the life and ministry of your local congregation, and will provide a useful backcloth for consideration of any church activities or structures. Although these steps are all quite practical and will help determine the nature and success of the project, they are not intended as a substitute for prayer. Throughout the process a listening attitude should be cultivated. Not just listening to the opinions of others but hearts actively tuned to hear the voice of God, accompanied by a willingness to respond to His promptings.

Know yourself. Know your Church. Know your Community. Know your action plan. Whilst the nature of knowledge is that it grows and therefore is never complete, that is insufficient reason for failing to try to know the community that surrounds our church. To gain that knowledge takes action, and out of it should come action as well. If we are to show, in ways that can be grasped, what the love of God actually means, these areas of research need to be carried out. Growing knowledge will stimulate our prayer, enable our social concern and evangelism to be more relevant, and cause us to be more sensitively identified with the community itself.

PART III

Action Plan

8

Ready for Launch

Now is the time to act! General trends in society, and
potential personal and church-based resources have
been examined. The need for specific knowledge of the
local community has been highlighted. It is now time
to make a start on identifying the needs that local people
feel.

A tempting short-cut would be to consult members
of your congregation for their opinion on the neighbourhood and leave it at that. Unlocking the congregation's insights is an important part of the process
but is not sufficient in itself. Impressions may be selective and sadly, many Christians don't interact with
those outside the church except on the most superficial of levels. Others will have stories to share that
come from a lifetime lived in the locality. They will
have seen changes over the years that have radically
altered the way the community looks and functions.
Therefore, their contribution will be more realistic
and helpful.

Starting with your *local church* is however a good idea
for four reasons. First it is generally useful to ask questions that stimulate thought and shake up preconcep-
tions to test how accurate they are. It could be assumed
that the church already has its finger on the pulse of
the community. That may be an incorrect assumption.
Bear in mind that what is significant is not just what is

known, but how that knowledge has been gained in the first place.

Next, if this exercise is to be a prelude to some form of corporate caring action by your church, it is essential to involve as broad a spectrum of the congregation as possible. When people have in some way played a part in putting together a project, they then find it much easier to own and support when under way.

Thirdly, it is sometimes painfully easy to develop a "them" and "us" approach in a local congregation. The inner circle are the ones with the knowledge and expertise, doing most of the significant tasks in the church. Others watch from the sidelines wondering what part they can play or having ceased to expect to have anything to offer. Locked away in such people can be a wealth of local colour and knowledge. Giving real opportunities to tell their stories and share insights can affirm those who have previously felt undervalued within the church. It can also enrich the process of getting to know your community.

The final reason is to do with tapping valuable resources and contacts that already exist in your midst. The prospect of embarking on a period of research can seem quite daunting, causing us to turn to the professionals in the congregation for help. You may have a doctor or social worker in your church who can put you in touch with the relevant people or information, but don't overlook others who are less obvious. Remember people such as home helps, school caretakers, doctors' receptionists and those who work in clerical positions in caring agencies. They themselves may not have all the information you need but can provide names, contacts and introductions to those who do. Be creative in your thinking in this area.

Depending on the size of the congregation methods vary concerning how to tap those insights and contacts. Pastoral visits and personal interviews in order to glean information are valuable but time consuming and so are best carried out in smaller churches. Some churches have circulated questionnaires amongst the congregation. These need to be brief and easy to understand, asking for both facts and impressions. Facts include details about length of time lived in the area and level of involvement, contacts with others caring in the community, useful names and addresses, and any other relevant information. Impressions, while obviously more subjective, assist in building up a fuller picture of what the neighbourhood is like. These can include questions about local problems, what sort of community spirit there is, and how the congregation think their particular church is viewed by those outside it.

The value of questionnaires can be limited because of the proportion of people who feel in some way threatened by them, see them as irrelevant or simply never get around to completing them. Therefore, careful preparation is needed. Thorough explanation before distribution, a realistic time limit for completion, and certain people given the responsibility of encouraging others to complete them on time can all help make this a more effective approach.

Another method that can be usefully employed is where there is an existing structure in the life of the church of home-based groups. There, a series of questions can be introduced to stimulate discussion concerning perceptions of the area. That can be highly informative. It can all serve to reinforce the fact that all of life is important. The tendency to compartmentalise life so that there's a special piece for church and for God can be challenged. Encourage people to tell their own stories from which you can glean insights that will contribute to the overall picture. In so sharing themselves, they too may experience affirmation for who they are and what they can contribute.

Violet had become a committed Christian late in life. She was in her fifties when she started attending the local Baptist Church, prompted to go by the inner ache caused by the premature death of her husband. Life for her took on a new dimension after a personal encounter with God. Her new-found relationship with Jesus Christ gave meaning, direction and reality in a way that she didn't always have words to explain. She faithfully attended the church but felt that she didn't quite fit in. She lacked the religious words that others used, and as a newcomer didn't understand the subtleties of history and prejudice that so often seemed to influence and complicate church practice. As a result, Violet felt that somehow she wasn't as good a Christian as others and wouldn't be until she became more fluent in the language of the church.

Meanwhile, she got on with her life outside in the community. She had been born and bred in the locality, not moving out of it even when she married. Local people knew Violet and she knew them. Generations of local families had grown up around her and she knew people's life histories like the back of her hand. She had always been an open-hearted woman, willing to listen and help practically, so others trusted her. She was a fund of local knowledge and deeply involved in a network of community relationships. The professional carers knew her because of her work as a foster parent in earlier years, and more recently for the caring support that she gave certain isolated elderly people.

Here was someone who felt inadequate as a Christian and that she had little to contribute in the life of her church. Yet she was at the hub of the local community. Maybe if that Baptist Church had had the wisdom to go through one of the exercises described earlier, such as the small group discussion about the needs of the area, they would have discovered what a special person they had in their midst in Violet. Meanwhile, she continued in her sense of inadequacy, overlooked by those who perhaps should have known better.

Moving on from enquiries within your church it is worth exploring what *other local churches* are doing. Some in the area may have already or be in the midst of going through a similar exercise. Following the publication of *Faith in the City* (the report of the Archbishop's Commission on Urban Priority Areas) came recognition of the value of parish audits. Consequently, many Anglican and other churches have pursued a series of investigations similar to those proposed in this book. Therefore, contact local churches to find out what they are doing. It may well be that some of the groundwork has been done for you by others or they can point you towards helpful sources of information. Maybe you can avoid duplication of effort by working in partnership together, pooling your general findings. Irrespective of whether you are from an Anglican Church, the Diocesan Social Responsibility Officer can be particularly worth consulting for information and a broader grasp of what is happening in the churches in the social concern sphere.

The next step is to move outside the church to contact those already involved in some caring capacity in the community. *Professionals* in secular, statutory and voluntary helping agencies will have different perspectives to offer, and may well be surprised at being approached. Outlined in Appendix III are details of relevant organisations to contact that can be found in most regions.

As well as surprise, you may be greeted with some suspicion. Some may regard it as a waste of time – or be a little threatened! Therefore, it is important to be clear in your own minds before you start about what you want to know and why. A helpful guideline in presentation is to start from the basis that your church has a commitment to be more fully involved in the life of the local community. Your concern is to identify gaps in provision so that you can complement rather than duplicate what is already being done. Stress that you have made as priorities consultation and thorough investigation before making decisions about a course of action.

Obviously, be careful to avoid using "religious" language as that can be both alien and off-putting. Also, ensure that you are clear beforehand about your motives for involvement because if the impression is given that your concern is exclusively to evangelise, you will gain little sympathy. Ask for recommendations of other people to talk to and sources of written information. Do remember, that in your approach to a particular agency they may see a means of fulfilling a special interest that they have. This could be because of the strategic location of the church building or because you have specific concerns similar to their own. An exciting prospect possibly, but wait until all the research has been completed before committing yourself!

Who do we approach in the capacity of "professionals"? There are those that we automatically think of as being already involved professionally in community care. Health visitors, doctors, social workers, members of the Police Force, area Youth Officer and the local Housing Officer all come into this category. Don't forget the range of voluntary caring agencies such as the Citizens' Advice Bureau, Samaritans, Marriage Guidance Council, and those specialising in working with particular groups like elderly or homeless people. Do consult them because, though it can take time that you may feel you can ill-afford to spare, the longer term rewards will be there. Information and insights that they provide can help, and useful contacts for the future are made. The beginnings of relationships can be formed which will provide a basis for assistance with your project in the future as well as a potential source of referrals.

In all this, don't overlook others involved in the community in different capacities. Very often it is the people who deliver the post or the milk who have shrewd insights. Local painters, decorators, plumbers and electricians have access to homes in a way that few of us normally have. Hairdressers often act as informal counsellors for their clients. Remember, too, that it is not always the general practitioners but their receptionists who are in touch with local issues and gossip. Take, and create, informal opportunities to learn from people like these as well as the professionals.

There are other methods of getting to grips with the neighbourhood. *General awareness* can be stimulated by keeping eyes and ears open. Local newspapers should be read regularly. The news items and chat shows on local radio can also be quite revealing. Be alert to notice advertisements and posters in public places that are advertising forthcoming community events. These can often be issue centred. Most libraries have displays and leaflet tables that give local information, so check these occasionally.

General *public opinion* is essential, albeit sometimes confusing! First, talk with people with whom you already have some contact. Shopkeepers, transport staff, and launderette attendants should be included in this category. Consult neighbours. Ask the opinion of those who cross your path at various activities such as playgroups or keep fit classes. It may well be that these enquiries will provide a platform for the beginnings of relationships with people that you formerly felt unable to approach.

THE COMMUNITY SURVEY

The most practical way of gauging public opinion is through conducting a community survey. This can be carried out in the local shopping area or on a house to house basis. The latter is more time-consuming but also more effective for relationship building. Be aware that not everyone will be able to give answers to your questions in the way you would expect. Some people will love to talk, perhaps because of being quite lonely, and will provide answers that can appear totally irrelevant.

On the other hand, some people are so unused to being asked their opinions about wider issues that they will have little to say. This is likely to occur more in run-down, socially and economically deprived neighbourhoods. However, it is crucial that the local community both feels, and is, consulted about local needs. Asking for an opinion communicates that the church considers people's viewpoints important enough to listen to. It is another means of ensuring that you are eventually responding in some way to felt local need.

Meanwhile, the thought of doing house to house visiting with a questionnaire can paralyse the average church member with fear and embarrassment. Their experience of such activities has normally been limited to overt evangelism which has, more often than not, been found to be an uncomfortable experience. However, the type of survey being recommended here is more focused on community need than people's impressions of the Christian faith. It takes the pressure off the interviewer to come up with "spiritual" answers, and so frees them to be more natural about their beliefs. The aim of the questionnaire is a genuine desire to find how the community functions and what the needs are that aren't being met. A positive spin-off from this can be opportunities to express the reasons for the church's concern but it would be unethical to use the softer approach of community needs merely as a vehicle for presenting the gospel. This is especially true where the church concerned has little intention of doing anything for the benefit of the community on the basis of the information that they are asking the public for.

A sample outline can be found in Appendix II of the

type of community needs questionnaire described here. Some churches prefer to compose their own so that they can focus on their particular concerns but you will find the sample basic and flexible enough for adaptation according to your requirements. One practical point about a survey. Those interviewed may, quite rightly, want to know what is going to be done with the gathered information. Creative thought should be given to this beforehand. Obviously, the main use is of an internal nature. However, it can be helpful to complete a summary of the findings to be printed as part of an article in the local newspaper or publicise the findings on a large bright poster outside the church. Again, it communicates that the public's opinion has been taken seriously, gives them a more comprehensive picture of what their community is like, and also provides a publicity springboard for the new caring project when it is eventually launched.

The benefits of a community survey therefore include communicating a positive message to local people, mobilising previously diffident church members and acquiring a deeper knowledge of the neighbourhood. There are two other gains to be had through using this approach. Some churches are criticised by local people for their lack of contact with the community. Christians may go in and out of the church building but nobody from outside ever has a conversation with them unless it's to complain about the insensitive car parking arrangements or excessive noise. Churches like that don't have a human face. However, by carrying out a survey they give local people the opportunity to actually meet them. Through this means, they have the chance of showing that they are really quite ordinary people, who

are growing into those with an extra-ordinary concern
for the community.

The other gain is of a longer term nature. By having
been thorough in the first place it is much easier to suc-
cessfully launch a new caring project. A platform for it
will have been built in asking for public opinion. This
could be especially true in situations where there has
been a clear response from locals, with the new project
being obviously a follow-up to that. Publicity can then
refer quite legitimately to the consultation and discussion process that had gone on in preparation.

Lastly, a cautionary note. A community survey, accompanied by promises of action, should not be undertaken unless there is a genuine commitment on the part
of the church to do something. A flurry of activity followed by deafening inaction will only serve to widen
the gap between church and community, deepening
mistrust of Christians, and stimulating scepticism about
the relevance of the Church today.

So far, you will have gained a bag of mixed impressions and some factual information. Valuable contacts
will hopefully have been made. Written *statistics and
reports* provide a different perspective. These can be
obtained from a variety of sources. A good starting place
is the Reference Library. They should have in their
possession copies of reports compiled by local authority
departments such as Planning, Education and Social
Services. Census details and a more locally relevant
breakdown of the figures, called Small Area Statistics,
should also be available. A useful, although not always
available resource is that of electoral ward profiles.
These consist of detailed statistical information about
small geographical areas in a borough or district.

Selective study of statistics can show shifts in population trends, where certain age groups are concentrated, and identify minority or special need groups within the community. Some indication of future trends can also be gleaned. Reports by departments such as Social Services often highlight key areas of need. If the library has limited details it is advisable to consult the Information Department within your local Town Hall. Bear in mind that voluntary caring agencies may also have compiled their own reports that could be useful to your research. You can track down these agencies through umbrella organisations such as the area Council for Voluntary Service.

By this stage, a lot of information will have come into your hands. A bewildering array of official reports, statistical information, muddled public opinion, and general impressions lie in front of you. Somehow, you have to make sense of it all and make the information accessible to others in the church.

Go through it all, picking out common strands of information. Identify the more obvious pockets of need, both geographically and socially. It will help you to do this if you work towards preparing a report for the church that will encompass the facts and impressions about local need. It will have to be easy to read, using pictures and charts, and a minimum of statistical details. If possible, also make the report available to those agencies and individuals that you've consulted from outside the church.

As well as a report, some sort of display put up in the church would enable those not directly involved to glimpse what's happening. Central to this should be a large map of the area, pinpointing significant places upon it. These could include social and recreation centres, caring organisations, official buildings, and other churches. An overall visual grasp can be quite important, enabling clearer understanding of the distribution of need and resources. The wider issue communication with the church about the project itself and the findings of your investigation will be explored in more detail in the next chapter.

* * *

One last word, a very simple but seldom thought of way of getting to know the community is that of getting out of the car and *walking around the area*. So much is missed when travelling by car. Lives dominated by meetings and haste fail to see what the community is like. Walk around the area slowly at different times of the day and the week. You'll find that the character of a place can change over the space of a few hours. And as you walk, pray. Consciously take Jesus with you, and in your imagination see Him there at your side. Ask Him to open your eyes to see what He sees, giving you His insight into the community. While you walk, ask Him to reveal His heart to you so that your concerns can reflect His. Pray that the influence of evil will be pushed back and His goodness released in the places where you walk. Covenant to co-operate with Him to that end.

9

Lift Off!

Questions have been asked, impressions gained and needs identified. All the strands have now to be drawn together, with the long months of investigation providing some focus for your church's future activity in the community. A definite course of action needs to be decided upon. What is going to be done, how it will be accomplished, and who is to be closely involved, are the next decisions to be faced. Careful thought should be given to these things because you are now entering a crucial phase.

The nature of the project you decide upon will determine the numbers and sort of people who have particular responsibility within it. Particular attention needs to be given to how those people will be trained and supported. Whatever size or type of community initiative you choose, a team approach is always to be recommended. Whether there are two, twelve or twenty people involved makes little difference to the value of working from a basis of team relationships. The means used to build those relationships may vary according to the numbers but the undergirding principles will remain the same.

Adopting a team structure will short-circuit many of the potential problems that can arise when rugged individualists are left to function largely in isolation from the mainstream of the local church and its leadership.

However, instead of concentrating on the negatives to be prevented, outlined below are several benefits to be gained from a team approach in community concern. There is potential for enormous mutual support and affirmation to be gained from working as part of a team. Entering into the pain and chaos of other people's life situations can be a draining experience. Inner conflicts can arise and the pressure of others' expectations cause emotional and spiritual weariness. Working with others within a climate of mutual openness and opportunity to express tensions is therefore important because of the measure of relief that it can bring. Team members can ease the load for each other and provide an informed listening ear when pressures build up. Unpleasant or distressing situations that are encountered can be shared in the knowledge that it is safe to do so and confidentiality will be maintained.

Much learning is best carried out in a group setting and a team of people with a common goal is particularly conducive to this. The level of motivation is often higher in a team context. Relationships can make it easier to learn new concepts and skills. It's easier to risk looking foolish in front of others when you know they are on your side! Training people thoroughly is time-consuming so doing so in a team setting maximises the benefit of available resources and mutual learning. Team members will also gain a lot from each other as they work, pray and plan together and in so doing learn on the job, often without realising it.

Shared vision and group identity are closely allied. There is strength in having a common purpose which is rooted in individually held convictions about God's agenda for the world. It can be a source of great joy to know that there are others alongside you who share your concerns and priorities. Individual perspectives and contributions are bound to vary but unity of purpose will create a strong bond. Group identity will evolve as the team works and learns together, and this is something to be positively aimed towards.

A danger to safeguard against is that of a brand of elitism or superiority emerging. The project team can have such a strong sense of belonging that they become a clique within the church, causing others to feel excluded. Whilst this cannot be altogether avoided because group identity is sometimes threatening to those who are not directly involved, it serves as a reminder that the vision behind the project should be owned by the bulk of the church membership. It is also essential that it's one that the whole church leadership identify with wholeheartedly, even if they are not involved at first hand.

A team approach should stimulate the growth and personal development of its members. This is not only brought about by providing training but also through opportunities that arise to use individual gifts and personality strengths. Having a team structure means that leadership can emerge and people get opportunities to try new things with a safety net of support beneath them. If there is shared responsibility more room is given for confidence to grow than when it all rests on one person. Review of team activities can enable individuals to take up new openings and others to let go of things that they are unsuited for.

Closely linked with this is accountability. Informal mutual accountability can be healthy and often functions well in a team setting. Clear lines of responsibility, with leaders committed to the nurture of all concerned, will ensure that individuals don't go off at such an extreme tangent that they expose either themselves or others to damage. Within a team structure, a delicate balance should always be aimed for, between a right level of accountability and the freedom to develop initiative. People need to know the security that comes from healthy obligations towards others and yet have space to try out new ideas.

Last but certainly not least, the public who make use of the project should get a better service if there is a team running it. Even if the team only consists of two people there will be differences of approach that could benefit those on the receiving end. In this way a variety of knowledge, skills and helpful contacts can be introduced to provide a better all-round service. Some personalities will be more suited to certain types of people than others, more easily establishing rapport. And with no one team member being particularly dominant it is less likely that those seeking assistance will become overtly dependent on an individual.

* * *

Teams don't just happen. It takes hard work and commitment to build a team but the rewards can be considerable. There are various ways in which one can be built but the first step is to decide what priority will be given to relationships. The option is whether to concentrate exclusively on the task and equipping people for it, or to introduce means by which the team can become more relationship centred. If opting for the former, then time spent together will be largely occupied by business and structured training input. The latter approach embraces needs for laughter and fun together, providing opportunities to mix socially and learn about different dimensions of each other than those just seen when at work. The latter emphasis is strongly recommended because it has potential for welding people together into a warm supportive unit that happily tolerates individual idiosyncracies and gives room for personal growth.

There are various different methods of team building. Time invested in individuals by the leadership is crucial. However, for the sake of brevity we'll concentrate here on group activities. The suggestions below can be adapted to apply to teams of different sizes and will obviously be affected by the type of project they're working on together. We can learn something from one particular church that ran an Advice Centre along the lines of a small scale Christian Citizens' Advice Bureau. Over a period of time they developed a range of activities that resulted in a strong team being established. These were largely introduced at the suggestion of team members and a regular process of consultation ensured that the team's felt needs were in some measure being met.

One such suggestion, much to the dismay of the team leader who didn't like getting up early, was that they should have a weekly prayer breakfast together. However, it did wonders for breaking down barriers as each saw what the others were like at 6.30 in the morning! Regular prayer together also confirmed vision and direction, with ripples of excitement caused by clear answers to prayer being seen.

Separate times of worship, prayer and Bible study were also important. They gave opportunity for corporate reflection upon the reasons undergirding the project. Principles for action could be thrashed out within a prayerful and Biblical framework and time could be spent waiting on God for specific guidance.

A pattern of regular team meetings devoted to planning and training was introduced. Everybody was encouraged to participate at some level in the planning. Training sessions utilized the different skills of those present and didn't rely merely on outside speakers. Training tended to be participatory in emphasis using discussion, role play, case studies, videos and games. In this way everybody could join in no matter what their level of experience. Any excuse to celebrate was taken, with meals and social activities being a regular feature. Barbecues and Sunday lunches were the most popular and drew in others who were not directly involved in the project but were linked by close association with particular team members.

And so a team was built. A group of people who gradually learned to trust each other; who laughed and cried and prayed together. The majority grew in confidence and maturity although some struggled along the way. Bonds of loyalty were strengthened and mutual encouragement became more common. Rough edges were chipped off and on occasions tempers became frayed. But through it all flowed the motivating power of the Holy Spirit, enabling a motley group of most unlikely people to take the love of Jesus out into the world.

* * *

PRACTICALITIES

A team approach is the key to the success of a church community care project. As well as that, however, there are certain principles and guidelines that are important to implement within the actual project if it is to run smoothly and effectively. These apply whether you are planning to set up a parents and toddlers group or a senior citizens lunch club, an unemployment project or a coffee morning. Whatever the size of the project, careful thought and preparation should go into the way that it's established.

The stories of two very different local churches provide us with helpful insights concerning those principles and guidelines. The first church is a small independent one, with a congregation of about thirty people. Their rather run-down and dingy looking old building is situated in an inner city area, surrounded by tower blocks of flats and few social amenities except for the local pub.

They moved from a survival mentality to begin to be more outward-looking. This led them to make some preliminary enquiries into local needs. They were profoundly moved by the sheer scale of what they uncovered, and consequently decided to examine in more depth what part they could play in the community, however small. Quite a lot of background research and consultation was carried out, including a selective door to door survey. As a result, they decided that what was needed was a debt counselling service. Their resources meant that it would have to be initially a small scale project but they were none the less determined to do things thoroughly.

Meanwhile, the second church also decided it was time to act. A member church of a mainline denomination, with a congregation of about eighty people, they had traditionally put more emphasis on internal church affairs rather than the local community. The focus had been on upgrading the church buildings, not on the needs of those outside the church. Influenced by trends and teaching within denominational circles they carried out a similar exercise to the first church. Having a more sizable and affluent congregation meant that they could be more thorough in their investigations and could afford to consider a more ambitious venture. They too attempted to identify the felt needs of the local community. Alongside this, they carried out a long overdue internal review that caused something of a rumpus but ultimately proved to be worthwhile. They concluded that a Crisis Helpline with a back-up befriending scheme would be invaluable. There was no such facility available in the area but there was every indication that one was needed.

Here are two different churches with separate types of initiative being established. However, the practical issues that they had to tackle were similar. First, they had to decide what their *aims* were. Who was to be assisted by the project and what did they expect to see accomplished? How would they measure failure or success? They had to ask themselves questions about the anticipated effects of their activities upon the community and whether this related to perceptions of their church at all.

Were they expecting people to be converted to Christ through contact with the project? Or was the emphasis to be upon a concern for a demonstration of the love and justice of God, with there being little or no explanation of the gospel? Was the focus to be upon short-term and crisis contact or longer term relationship building? How far were they to take the initiative in running things themselves and at what level, if at all, would they be prepared to work in partnership with non-Christians? All these and other questions related to their aims had to be addressed by both churches. You likewise will need to be clear about your aims and expectations, no matter what sort of initiative you are involved with.

Following on naturally came the need to do some thinking about the *limits and boundaries* of the different projects. The first church had decided upon a narrowly defined area of work and some natural limits for involvement were already built in. People struggling with debt might well have other areas of difficulty but the church decided that they were neither equipped nor able to offer any other form of assistance. Therefore, they had to formulate some guidelines for the workers that incorporated these boundaries. These were determined by the expertise and resources available, with it being acknowledged that they would need regular review because of changing circumstances. The second church also had to grapple with how far they should go with those who approached them for help. The facility that they planned to offer the community was quite general and unfocused. Any sort of problem with varying degrees of complexity could come their way. For them it was therefore particularly important that they be clear about what skills and knowledge they could provide.

Both churches also had to do some homework in finding out the best places to refer people on to for more specialised aid than they themselves could give. This would make it easier to turn down a request for help that lay outside of their experience and would ensure that people were at least pointed in the right direction.

The smaller church tried to lay down some guidelines about the volume of work they could cope with by specifying the maximum number of people to be seen during the course of a week. This proved to be helpful but when reviewed in the light of experience a few months later, had to be adapted to a more realistic level. This in turn led them to set up an appointment system as a means of controlling the demand.

How to maintain a Christian ethos and the limits that this would impose on the range of their work was also talked about by both churches. Neither came to firm conclusions before the respective projects were launched but a commitment was made to regularly review the issue. They opted to tackle things as they arose but it may well be that you should consider establishing clear boundaries before you start.

An example of clear-cut boundaries being built into a church project from the outset can be found on the south coast of England. There a Centre has been set up providing free pregnancy testing and counselling help for those with unwanted pregnancies. They decided from the outset that they would not assist women in obtaining abortions. They do however help people think through the implications of different courses of action and also offer counselling to those who have already gone through the trauma of abortion. This is the limit that they perceive as being laid down by their Christian convictions. It should be noted that within the implementation of that limit they attempt to ensure that realistic and supportive alternatives to abortion are offered.

Returning to the two churches described earlier and their planning of community care projects, there came a parting of the ways in their thinking about boundaries to observe. Levels of expertise, the volume of work that could be coped with, and how to establish a Christian ethos had been considered by both. The smaller church, in setting up a debt counselling service, went on to explore ways in which they could make sure that they weren't doing everything on behalf of those seeking help.

Their concern was to enable people to grow in confidence and ability to tackle debt problems themselves. They saw their work as being preventative in its long-term effects as well as providing relief in the short-term. In practice, this meant that they encouraged "clients" to take responsibility for their actions and taught them skills in letter writing and telephone negotiations. Sensitivity to the individual was obviously strategic to the effectiveness of this policy.

Initially, the other church gave no thought to this at all. They had quite a large and competent team of workers who tended to think in terms of doing things for people because they needed help. It was not until some time after the Helpline had got under way that they began to realise that they were creating some unhealthy over-dependent relationships with those who used it. Several of their workers were floundering under the pressure of unrealistic demands placed upon them. A radical rethink had to take place and some of the team had to learn that saying "no" to a request can sometimes be the most constructive course of action to pursue.

Another practical consideration that these two churches had to face, was that of *follow-up contact.* You likewise, will need to explore how that fits in, if at all, with the type of community involvement you are planning. Your understanding of how overt evangelism relates to the project will obviously influence this. The two churches tackled it in different ways, influenced in this by their size of congregation and available resources. The members of smaller church were painfully aware that they had insufficient people for effective individual follow-up visits. They tackled the problem creatively and devised a two-pronged approach.

First, they strove to ensure that priority was given to there being space for the personal touch in all that was done in their small Money Advice Centre. People who came in were always to be treated as being of worth. Where possible, time was given to each one to cover in more depth their needs and aspirations. Cups of coffee or tea, with biscuits, were always offered. People were addressed by name and given a warm handshake on departure. This effectively reduced the number of people they could spend time with but they held to the conviction that the quality of response was important. The stigma of debt can considerably undermine human dignity and this was something they wanted to counteract in some measure through caring practice.

Secondly, three people were given responsibility for organising regular social activities. These were to be for the whole church and suitable for inviting new people to join in with. Alongside this, every effort was made to make sure that existing church activities were flexible and relevant enough to receive newcomers in a positive fashion. Lack of resources had hindered them in their desire to offer individual support to people. However, instead of giving up and doing nothing, they tried to create structures of welcome and care that would enable responsibility to be widely shared amongst the small church community.

The leadership of the larger denominational church concluded that personal befriending and support of those contacted through the Helpline was very important. However, as it was quite a large church they left it to the project leader to draw in church members when they were needed. It was thought that matching people by age and background was important but other than that no new structure for follow-up was established. There was a sufficiently large pool of people to draw upon as necessary.

This informal approach proved to be something of a problem. The leader spent an inordinate amount of time trying to identify church members who were both suitable and willing to help out at short notice. Several that did agree had to be chased up to ensure that they visited promptly. Others that faithfully fulfilled their responsibility were often themselves left feeling isolated and unsupported as they tried to get alongside people in quite dire situations.

After six months of working in this way, the glaring inadequacies could no longer be avoided. Something had to be done that would provide more structure, direction and support for those involved. Besides this, the

issue of how to ensure that confidentiality was maintained had to be dealt with. Their response was to ap-
point a follow-up team with two leaders who had
pastoral responsibility for them. Team members were
drawn from a cross section of ages and backgrounds but
all had some ability to be sensitive to the needs of others.
Everyone involved worked in a spare-time capacity.
They received training and participated in regular re-
views of their follow-up relationships with a team leader
so that a sense of direction could be maintained. Con-
fidential matters were kept within the confines of the
team and so both client and worker were protected.

Not everyone who contacted the Helpline needed or
requested a follow-up visit but those who did received,
on the whole, a much better standard of care after the
team was formed. In situations where the Helpline
didn't have sufficient expertise to fully respond, members of the follow-up team could still offer ongoing support. Contacts in these situations would be referred on
to other agencies for specialised help with a team member still offering befriending. The introduction of this
team structure proved invaluable and was used in many
instances to more meaningfully "flesh out" the gospel.

Obviously, there were a lot of practicalities that both
of these churches had to cover besides those of aims,
boundaries, and follow-up. Issues related to buildings,
personnel, finance, and timing are all pertinent. Both
churches were sensible enough to build into their structures room for *flexibility* and opportunity for *review*.
There should always be enough flexibility in organisational structures to allow for the unexpected and to create a climate for growth. Review is necessary if
God-given objectives are to be kept at the forefront and

faithfulness to His purposes for the community are to be pursued.

These two churches differ considerably but even so may bear little resemblance to your situation. That doesn't really matter, in that the questions and issues that they grappled with in preparation for the launch of their community projects are essential pieces of scaffolding for the building of any social concern initiative. Many potential problems were prevented, and whilst not all aspects could be immediately pinned down in detail, they had created the means by which everything important would eventually be covered. You too, need to consider the principles that they strove to incorporate so that your church involvement in the community may effectively demonstrate the reality of God's love for hurting people.

* * *

In order to make sure that lift off of the new project goes smoothly and has the maximum impact in the right quarters, attention needs to be given to effective communication. This is something that churches tend not to be very good at. This is because it is not given high enough priority or there is diffidence about being too image conscious. The object of good communication is to make certain that people are enabled to grasp the essentials and so give full support. This applies equally inside the church as it does to the local community.

It has already been stressed that it is crucial to gain as much support from within the church as possible for any community initiatives that are undertaken. It is important that what is done is owned by the congregation and so given their support. If the project is to be one expression of that body of Christians' commitment to the locality then they need to understand what it is about. Their prayers, interest and contributions will be needed in order to make it a success.

Information can be passed by word of mouth but a permanent visual display situated inside the church building is particularly useful. Put up a large map of the area with significant buildings such as schools, caring agencies and social centres clearly marked. Indicate what the church's parish or catchment area is and show by use of pie or bar charts what proportion of different groups of people there are within the area. To make it more attractive put some recent photos alongside the map to illustrate what the area is like. Church members may be familiar with the neighbourhood but this can help to bring it more alive to them as being of significance to the church's ministry. Remember that incomers to the church will also see the display so make sure that there is nothing potentially offensive on it to those who are not committed Christians. If you are ready to do so, you could also display details of the new project. This could take the form of a brief description, samples of publicity that will be used, and photographs of all the team members.

Church members may well have questions and doubts about what is being proposed and it is therefore important to create opportunities for these to be aired and responded to. If you have home groups these can be a good forum for a more relaxed exploration of issues. Depending on the number of groups the project leader or other team members could visit each one prior to the launch so that anxieties can be allayed and misinformed prejudices dispelled. Thorough exposure should be given to the project through church services. Be imaginative in this. Perhaps you could use drama and a slide presentation, as well as Biblical teaching concerning the mandate to be "salt and light" in society. Use any means of communication that are available to you and in that way the information should filter through to most people.

Communication shouldn't stop once things are under way. People will need regular imaginative updates in order to keep the project near the forefront of their thinking and their prayers. Make sure that the information on display inside the church is up to date and looks bright and eye-catching. Scruffy, out of date details communicate a negative impression. If there is a church magazine insert occasional articles on the work of the project. Maintain a reasonably high profile through regular contributions to services and providing non-confidential information for prayer. Don't forget to communicate the answers to prayer when they come as well!

Try to visit the home groups at least once a year in order to give continued opportunity for questions and dialogue about the project. Lastly, compile an annual report for circulation to all interested parties. This will help discipline you to assess what has been happening, and will provide valuable information for the leaders and members of the church. If your church is one that has a significant proportion of non-readers then make sure that the report is as brief and visual as possible, using pictures and charts to communicate the main points. Visual content is generally helpful, no matter who is reading the report.

Publicity outside the church needs careful thought.

What you use will project an image and you should be sure of what you are trying to get across to the community. Consistency is very important so that the public can begin to identify which activities are to do with your church. This can be achieved by adopting a distinctive logo or symbol to go on all publicity, signs and letter headings. Choose a particular colour for leaflets and posters that will be used for all publicity associated with the project. Try to pick an unusual colour but ensure that it is likely to continue to be available. Admittedly, written publicity methods will be governed by the type of project and available budget but general publicity could include large eye-catching posters situated in public places such as the library, doctor's surgery, local launderette and shops, and popular pubs. Try to get them put up in official buildings such as the Police Station, D.H.S.S., offices of the Registrar of Births, Deaths and Marriages, Housing Department, Social Services and other statutory and voluntary agencies. Hopefully, the way will have already been paved for this during your earlier months of community research and relationship building.

The premises should be made accessible and clearly visible to those seeking them out or just passing by. Put up a large and boldly lettered permanent sign which can be seen from several angles. Don't forget that the logo should also be on it. Write letters of introduction to all local caring agencies and churches explaining what is being done and building upon previous contact.

If possible, get some attractive leaflets printed for distribution throughout the locality and for general ongoing use. Try including, in bold letters, wording to the effect that the leaflet shouldn't be thrown away because the information would be useful in the future. Shortage of people to help may mean that it's difficult to deliver the leaflets to local households. If this is the case, it is sometimes possible to negotiate delivery through a newsagent's paper round. Whilst this may be an option it should only be pursued if you really cannot deliver them yourselves.

Finally, depending on whether the size of the project warrants it, there could be a proper launch event. If opting for this course of action you should plan it in advance, inviting a well-known personality to formally open the project. Newspaper coverage should be explored. Whether or not there is an official "lift off", it may be possible to get a feature included in the newspaper that incorporates the findings of the public opinion survey and links it with the new project. This will not only publicise the project but will also communicate the church's desire to listen to local people.

After all this is done and the project is well under way, publicity cannot then be forgotten. Efforts have to be made to ensure that posters and leaflets are kept up to date and look reasonably attractive. If local people feel that they can have some confidence in you they will approach you for assistance. Part of that confidence building is achieved in communicating a warm but efficient image through publicity. Don't forget to keep a high profile with other agencies through the use of annual reports or regular updates, as well as appropriate ongoing contact.

Efforts at ensuring good communication are never wasted so although this may seem a lot of work it will reap valuable long term effects. It is not meant to be a substitute for prayer and actually getting on with the job of expressing God's care, but it is an integral part of enabling the church to become effectively involved with the needs of its surrounding community.

Know Your God

To know, and be known, by at least one other significant individual is crucial to emotional wellbeing. Think about the people in your life that you could reasonably confidently say that you know. That knowledge will be made up of several strands.

First, there are certain facts. Ones to do with age, physical description, place of birth, current residence and main occupation. As well as this, you'll have some understanding of what that individual is like as a person. Their attitudes, feelings and reactions will be familiar and often predictable. Those unique personality quirks that might startle others, hold few surprises for you. The more intimate your knowledge the more fully you understand their aspirations. What causes pain or brings joy is obvious. You are acquainted with what really matters to that person.

In turn, this knowledge affects your responses within the relationship. Your expectations are influenced and with a deepening closeness you can gain a reasonably accurate picture of what that person has to offer you. Their inner resources and strengths may not be immediately obvious to others but you will know just how far you can rely upon them. But however complete you think your knowledge is there will always be more to discover.

That is the awesome nature of human relationships.

And there are parallels to be found in our relationship with God. He too can be known, wants to be known, and there is always more to explore. His thoughts, His feelings, and His agenda for the world are central to an intimate understanding of Him. More than that, breathtakingly true is the fact that within our relationship with Him, who He is, with all His power, is made generously available to us.

Knowing God is the cornerstone for Christian social concern. Not just head knowledge, nor purely experience, but a potent blend of the two. In-depth research of the community, and radical appraisals of the church have their place. They are important but not enough. It is God Himself who makes the difference. What we initiate in the community, how it is outworked and the reasons behind it all come back to knowing God. If what we do as individuals and corporately is in the name of Christ, then a priority has to be that of gaining a deepening personal knowledge of Him. Then we can more fully reflect His concerns and draw upon His resources in all that we do.

KNOW YOUR MESSAGE

You need a theology of mission before you do your final planning. Time needs to be given to working on a growing understanding of the sheer magnitude of God's purposes for the world. Where have we come from and what are God's intentions for the future of humankind? Explore the wonder of it on a grand scale and then focus in on to the implications for you and your immediate neighbourhood.

The Bible is packed with references to the future for God's people. There are vivid scenes of joy and celebration, a bringing together of all peoples no matter what their background. Relationships are characterised by justice and trust. There is freedom for all and wholeness is denied to no one. All death, evil, oppression and suffering have been banished. Righteousness abounds. Creation in all its splendour is restored. The peace of God which transcends understanding seems to be in the very atmosphere.

A superb picture of what is promised with radical implications for now. We are called to participate with God in bringing in this future. His purposes are to become our purposes. His agenda for the world is to be reflected in what we do in our locality. It is not enough to be stirred by human need – important though it is to have compassion. It is not enough to listen to and be influenced by the mainstream of the church moving towards greater social involvement – important though it is to hear what the Spirit is saying to the Church in this generation. We ourselves need to be so gripped by an understanding of present realities and a vision for the future that they become the bedrock for action.

This should be worked on amongst the leadership of your church and taught to the congregation before setting up a community initiative. It will need teaching in such a way that something of the facts about God and His purposes are grasped. A theological framework is necessary for sense to be made of the project and understanding of how it fits into the mission of the church. However, true knowledge of a person, whilst informed by facts, comes from intimate interaction. So it is between God and His people. Both the leadership and the congregation need to meet with God in order for those facts to come alive.

This is particularly important for those who will be directly involved in the initiative but also for the rest of the church so they can own it as theirs too. If you are reading this as a person who on your own wants to do something, because as yet your church doesn't share your ambitions, then these principles equally apply. Persevere in discovering a theology of mission and seek God so that He can make it real to you.

Developing a Christian mind on matters should be an ongoing process for individuals and teams involved in social concern projects. Every effort ought to be made to prepare workers to respond "Christianly" to issues that will arise. Not all eventualities can be covered beforehand and many are best dealt with as they occur. Thought therefore needs to be given to ways in which learning can happen both before and during the lifetime of the project.

In the course of a week a church-based Advice or Care Centre could be faced with a fourteen-year-old girl with an unwanted pregnancy, an unemployed man fiddling the D.H.S.S. and a distressed single parent who in desperation has broken into the gas meter. That could be either a good or a bad week, depending on how you look at it! That's without mention of the squatters, those with a homosexual lifestyle, or people involved in adulterous relationships who may come seeking advice about their rights.

All these people, and more, will need responses that are informed by Christian principles and undergirded by Christlike compassion. Therefore, a structure for regular discussion and training related to ethical issues will be necessary for all the workers. If this sounds too high-powered don't be put off. The principle is that of ensuring that opportunity is given to develop a Christian mind. What form this takes will vary according to the type of project adopted and the people involved. However, if the church leadership want their congregation to be growing in social awareness, and they themselves to be more supportive to the project workers, then efforts should be made to tackle such concerns.

Close knowledge of a person and time spent with them usually affects us. We pick up some of their mannerisms, and their values can become ours or at least in some measure influence the way we behave. In a similar manner if we are to be effective as "salt and light" in the community, then increasingly our values need to reflect those that are upon God's heart.

This, like developing a Christian mind, is a growing and ongoing process. It is an individual responsibility and yet also can have corporate outworkings. As we saw earlier, the quality of communal life within the church can make a vivid impact, whether for good or harm, upon the visitor. The things that we hold dear are often more obvious to them than they are to us.

Knowing God has implications for our lifestyle and the things that we consider important. This is relevant here because who we are can never be totally divorced from what we do. It is sometimes easier to disguise our individual values and resultant lifestyles when part of a larger church-based project. However, whilst this may be so, these things have a way of making themselves visible. This isn't about heinous crimes or sexual immorality, although obviously it can be applied to them. It is more to do with having life values that reflect those of Jesus as seen in the gospels. It is about incarnating Christ in all that we do and not just confining it to the particular hours of the week devoted to social concern.

If the dominant values of our culture of materialism and individualism rule our lives then our response to those in need is likely to be insensitive or patronising. We should, as individuals, be able to honestly identify ourselves with those who hurt without having to compartmentalise our lives. Corporately, the ethos of the project should communicate the life-giving and outwardly ministering values of Christ. That doesn't necessarily mean that material possessions have to be given away or that we should live in community before we can express the love of God in action. But it does have something powerful to say about motives and attitudes. To know God means that our values should increasingly reflect His.

Finally, if you have not done so already, you need to consider what the relationship will be in your community project between social concern and evangelism. This is only really possible when you are clear about what the project is to be, although obviously your understanding of the relationship between the two will influence the type of project you set up. It is helpful to have discussed this so that there are no false expectations placed upon or held within the project team.

This involves clarifying what place an explanation of the gospel will have when relating to those seeking help. How overtly Christian should the whole project be? Will it ever be deemed appropriate to pray with those who come in? Does the gift of healing have any part to play? Such questions need setting within the broader context of the overall aims and objectives of the project. It will obviously be affected by what sort of project it is and which sector of the community it is geared towards. For example, a Marriage Counselling Centre or Telephone Helpline might well be more overt about their Christian ethos than a government-funded unemployment project based on church property.

The decision about where evangelism fits in is not irrevocable. There should be room for flexible practice within given guidelines, and regular review of the emphasis when the project is under way.

SENSE OF DIRECTION

The different stages of enquiry, outlined in previous chapters, overlap and therefore are not written about in chronological order. Likewise, the subject matter of this chapter has application through the different stages, and whilst important now, should not be confined to when all the groundwork has been completed.

There needs to have been an attitude of listening to God, looking to Him for insight and clarity of perception. However, when the different preparation stages have been completed the time will come to make firm decisions about what to do. Hopefully, you now have a reasonably comprehensive and accurate picture of the local community. There is some understanding of local needs and aspirations, as well as projected shifts in populations trends. Alongside this, you are aware of various under-utilised church resources, including people whose potential in the social concern field has so far been largely untapped. Work has been going on to review existing activities, and already prayer and planning are in progress to facilitate a deepening of communal life within the church.

What have you got? Lots of information and possibly several ideas. Maybe a particular project has already emerged that seems practical to pursue. However, before going any further you need to know what God wants. You have to have the confidence that what is being planned is what God has in mind for your church or for you as a person. Bright ideas may abound but God-given direction is essential. Because of this, there should be at some point a special time set aside for actively seeking God, waiting on Him for direction. This is important for the leadership of the church and in some instances should include the whole congregation.

There will always be more needs than one person or group can ever hope to tackle. The sheer diversity of opportunity for intervention can be bewildering. Throughout Jesus' ministry He was pressed in on every side by people wanting Him to do something. Not all had their needs met. He seemed to have an unerring sense of knowing where to be at a given time, and with whom to get involved. It is that same purposefulness that is needed within the local church's strategy for community concern.

That can only be gained by spending time with God. One method is for the leadership to commit themselves to fast on a particular day. Operating within the constraints of their jobs, they spend time in prayer when they would normally be eating. At the end of the working day they meet together for worship and prayer. If they haven't had opportunity to walk around the church's neighbourhood as earlier recommended, then this should be done prior to praying together. It will sharpen the focus of attention and bring alive something of God's perspective on the community – how He sees it and His heart for the people. When the leaders come together, time should be spent asking God for wisdom and direction. Worship is integral to this. It also helps to be quiet as a group before God, and so make room for Him to speak. Following the time of prayer, a meal could be eaten together as an act of fellowship and celebration. People will have had opportunity to ponder before God what the issues are and discussion can then take place within the relaxed atmosphere of a meal about the next steps to take. The exercise could be repeated at regular intervals until such time as a clear direction emerges. Prior to this special day, everyone would need to have been fully briefed, probably in written form, concerning the needs, opportunities and possible resources. Presumably, some attention will also have been given beforehand to the leaders' corporate understanding of the theological basis for action. All this is then brought to God during that day for clarification and specific guidance.

This type of approach is invaluable in welding together a leadership team and does help bring about a sense of corporate vision for action. It is not meant to be a substitute for personal reflection or intercession but when added, contributes the stimulating dimension of a range of insights. The practice of fasting, prayer and meditation within a framework of Biblical and community awareness is equally important for the individual pursuing their own sense of calling. Also bear in mind that when your project is established, review times could include this sort of exercise.

CLIMATE OF FAITH

It is essential to stop within all the business of planning in order to be reminded of who God is. Unfortunately, activity can all too easily supercede relationship with Him. Necessary and worthwhile pursuits can relegate the enormity of God to the fringes of our mind. Reflect upon these words:

> This is what the Lord says – Israel's King and Redeemer, the Lord Almighty: I am the first and I am the last; apart from me there is no God. Who then is like me? Let him proclaim it. . . . Is there any God besides me? No, there is no other Rock; I know not one. (Isaiah 44:6-8)

As His voice thunders out afresh from the pages of Isaiah all our plans are brought into their rightful place. Where we have been in danger of becoming inflated with self-importance, the assertion of His identity reminds us again of who we are. When plans go awry or pressures threaten to overwhelm, the recollection of His supremacy over all things brings back perspective.

Time and again down through the centuries, God's people have been urged to recall who He is. In that sense, nothing has changed. We too are confronted with a God who is too large to overlook, with claims too stupendous to ignore. One such instance in the Bible is when Isaiah said to the people of the time:

> Here is your God! See, the Sovereign Lord comes with power. . . . He gathers the lambs in His arms,

and carries them close to His heart. Do you not know? Have you not heard? Has it not been told you from the beginning? Have you not understood since the earth was founded? He sits enthroned above the circle of the earth, and its people are like grasshoppers. He will not grow weary, and his understanding none can fathom. He gives strength to the weary and increases the power of the weak. (Isaiah 40:9-29)

These extracts vividly portray a God who is greater than we can imagine, possessing more power than we can comprehend. Yet there is a quality of tenderness in His care for the vulnerable that tugs at the heart-strings. This is our God whom we are called to know and to serve. It is this God that has given us the inestimable privilege of working with Him in the world to see His purposes for good become reality.

Growing awareness of what He is like can radically affect the different stages suggested in this book. For instance, attempts to gain greater self-knowledge conducted within a climate of faith in such a God can be a gloriously liberating experience. Instead of despairing at personal failings we can face them honestly in the knowledge that God is big enough to deal with them. There is a sense of safety in knowing that He understands our weakness, and has compassion on us without glossing over wrong attitudes or behaviour. The pathway to wholeness is offered us through repentance and renewal. Without knowing what He is like and able to do, attempts at self-improvement can be both inadequate and depressing!

Some find community research an absorbing pursuit.

There is so much to find out and endless successions of people to see. A kaleidoscope of impressions bombard the senses. One can feel almost assaulted by the rawness of the pain of others. Or maybe the apathy that pervades the neighbourhood atmosphere begins to dull the researcher's enthusiasm. The bright light of vision becomes obscured by others' disinterest. In moments such as these there is necessity to turn again to God for redirection and empowering. And we need to know what sort of a God it is to whom we turn.

Then, when it comes to an appraisal of the local church some of us will need particular trust in God. Sadly, some churches have become bastions against change. Fixed ideas and procedures may have become more important to the congregation than the adventure of faith. Those in leadership have responsibility to highlight wrong priorities and gently push for change; that can be a costly and sometimes lonely road to follow, so a large vision of God is essential to maintain.

Alternatively, there may be many signs of hope in the church. Growth is happening and an appraisal slots easily into a process of change that is already under way. Few feel threatened by it and many are excited. Here also, a clear vision of God and the centrality of faith in Him needs to be stuck to. We still need to keep returning to Him and checking out that we're going in the right direction. Let it be the Spirit of God that sets the pace rather than the momentum of success or enthusiasm.

Whatever your present understanding and expression of Christian social responsibility let these words speak to you, let them become central to your life:

Be still and know that I am God. I will be exalted
among the nations, I will be exalted in the earth.
The Lord Almighty is with us. (Psalm 46:10, 11)

Knowing God can never be a purely academic exercise
if we are committed to going beyond theory to experience. Inevitably, there are implications for our lives because He is a God who acts. He is on the move, working
towards the climax of human history. We can join in
the action but to do so is costly. It is also very exciting
and will be life-transforming. It means that as we venture out of the Christian ghetto into the local community to show God's love, we are going to need all the
resources that He makes freely available to us.

Volumes have been written down through history on
the variety of God's provision for His people. Active
caring requires particular God-given resources. People
seldom fit into the neat pigeon-holes that we create for
them. There is a delightful complexity about human
beings that can also frustrate and confuse us when
trying to assist. Matters in other people's lives can seem
perfectly clear to us with there being various logical
courses of action to follow. However, in practice it is
not usually that simple. Prejudices, eccentricities, and
distorted reasoning may influence behaviour far more
than calmly worked out logic. Emotional pain and spiritual oppression can cause all sorts of negative responses in the people that we are alongside.

Involvement in the lives of others can sometimes
leave us facing perplexing situations. Inner conflict
about how best to assist a particular person may well
arise. *Wisdom* is needed in order to respond rightly.
True wisdom is not just using carefully chosen words

and giving the correct answers. We may have the facts at our fingertips but what will be distinctive about a Christian's care is the use of supernatural wisdom, drawing it from God himself.

Spiritual wisdom is described in the Bible as being something more than providing solutions:

> . . . the wisdom that comes from heaven, is first of all pure; then peace-loving, considerate, submissive, full of mercy and good fruit, impartial and sincere. (James 3:17)

These are quite a catalogue of qualities. They considerably broaden the concept of wisdom. Whilst using Biblical commonsense, and bringing experience and knowledge together to apply to a given situation are included, it is also more than that. The true wisdom described in this verse is what we see in Jesus as He dealt with people. He displayed spiritual insight intermeshed with attitudes that reflected God's character.

Aiming to possess a radical cutting edge, tempered with compassion, with which to make a difference in the community requires the resource of spiritual wisdom. And the good news is that God has promised it to us!

> If any of you lacks wisdom, he should ask God, who gives generously to all without finding fault, and it will be given to him. (James 1:5)

There is probably common agreement within Christian circles that love is an essential ingredient when working amongst those in need. Not a sentimental or romantic type of love but a tangible quality that actively reaches out to others in an affirming way. It is something essentially creative and can be costly to those who are doing the giving. If we are to serve God in the world, then we need a baptism of love from God. We need His love pulsating through our veins bringing life to others. This should be a high priority for all those particularly active in one way or another as "salt and light".

However, complacency can creep in and we can begin to coast along, depending on stale resources or our own strength of personality. Consider Andy's experience. He spent several evenings each week at a project for homeless men. Many of them had been on the streets for years, while others were more recently discharged long-term psychiatric patients who'd fallen through the State's after-care safety net. A lot of them had alcohol-abuse associated problems and several were difficult to relate to. None the less, Andy was quite popular among them. He had a ready smile and a generous fund of jokes that could sometimes ease the tension in potentially explosive situations. Others in his church envied Andy his relaxed manner and ability to do that sort of work. They often commented on it and he enjoyed their admiration despite professing modesty.

Everything went along much as usual until one day a man came into the project who looked and smelled dreadful. This was nothing out of the ordinary but for some reason Andy found him repugnant. On closer acquaintance, Andy's dislike grew and he found himself avoiding the man whenever possible. The man seemed to sense this and go out of his way to make Andy aware of his presence. The situation continued with tension growing inside Andy. His smile became more forced and his jokes, although previously sometimes sarcastic, now became positively acid.

This was no ordinary problem related just to that one man. After a rather unpleasant blow-up in front of everybody, Andy was helped by the team leader to see that his reactions were symptomatic of something else. Gradually, he realised that for months he had been coasting along, going through all the outward motions of care and niceness. His naturally outgoing personality had helped carry him through, and he had managed to fool himself as well as others. Complacency had set in and any vestige of God-given love had evaporated. There had been nothing wrong in being paid compliments by his church contemporaries but his attitude in accepting them had only served to reinforce the complacency.

Then someone had stirred everything up. There is a Bible verse that exhorts us to offer hospitality to strangers and in so doing maybe we'll entertain an angel without knowing it (Hebrews 13:2). Perhaps the man who pestered Andy was a heavily disguised angel! Whoever he was, Andy was provoked to the point where he was confronted with his lack of love. He chose to return to God, who is described as love, admitting his poverty of spirit, and receiving a fresh infusion of supernatural love. He also learned to keep going back to God so that what he offered others continued to be vital and alive.

What about *opposition*? Not a resource from God but something that clamours for His provision to deal with it. There are spiritual realities that in our humanity we cannot as yet fully comprehend. There are forces of evil, supernatural powers, at work in this world and committed to undermining or destroying any activity of God. Where He brings love and freedom, they bring hostility, bitterness, fear and bondage. His purpose is to create life and wholeness. In contrast, where there is destruction or brokenness evil powers have in some way been at work.

The people of God are called to engage in battle against evil. For this, increasing discernment is essential, as well as appropriation of God's resources. When Christians get involved in care in society they are in one sense moving into the front line of battle. It is not particularly because our society is inherently more wicked than anywhere else. It is rather that as Christians take God's love and life to people, challenging injustice and oppression in its different guises, we will encounter evil forces opposed to what we're doing. The form that opposition will take can vary greatly from temptation to compromise on our part to undisguised antipathy from others.

Every time you meet someone who is trapped in deprivation that denies their personhood or involved in relationships fraught with bitterness and pain, you can be sure that is the position in which Satan wants them to remain. There is also evil to be found in society's structures which deny human dignity, perpetuate the myth that things matter more than people, or practices that are built on values that in no way reflect God's character. These things should be recognised and responded to for what they are. Discernment is necessary in order to do this.

Coming down to everyday application, this doesn't mean that everything which fails to go to plan is attributable to Satan. Neither does it mean that people opposed to what you are doing are necessarily agents of evil. They may sometimes be making a point that we should heed. What it does mean, however, is that we need to learn to recognise the demonic at work in particular circumstances. Prayer is central to this. Prayer, with a generous mix of worship and action, is also the means by which we counter evil. Therefore, our involvement with hurting people requires determined and positive intercession for them.

Within the closing chapters of the Book of Daniel is a small phrase that gives a clue to the key for successful opposition to Satan. The context is a prophecy in which evil is described as running rampant, being blatant in its power. In response the verse says, "but the people who know their God shall firmly resist."

The resources of God are limitless but there is one that is particularly applicable here, that of *joy*. One of the fears that churches entertain about community concern is that they will be overrun by people with problems. Their anxiety is that somehow they will be swamped, and there will be more for them to cope with than they either want or can handle. Wrong attitudes may abound but the fears are genuine and in some measure are rooted in possibility. God's love is attractive and does draw the bruised and battered from within society.

There are ways described in the previous chapter of ensuring that the church doesn't take on more than it can responsibly deal with. However, association with other people's pain can be difficult. Those with greater involvement are likely to experience at first hand the pressure and demands of that pain. A high degree of exposure can lead to feelings of stress and being overloaded. Other pressures may be added, such as people's unwillingness to comply with what we think is best for them, which while sometimes necessary can be disheartening. The inflexibility of bureaucratic organisations can be frustrating. And however understandable the reasons, the occasional inability to assist someone can lead to a sense of personal failure.

Whilst every effort should be made to support project workers and ensure that they don't become overloaded, the resource of supernatural joy still has an essential role to fulfil. A sense of inward celebration of God's goodness. Assurance of the purposes of God for human beings and an awareness of our own particular contribution. Confidence in the character of God and His ability to provide. These all belong as parts of that inner quality of joy that motivates and strengthens, and enables stickability through the most troubled circumstances. This is confirmed by the words of Nehemiah: "the joy of the Lord is your strength" (Nehemiah 8:10).

Sometimes we limit joy to bubbly effervescence or a perpetual smile. It may be expressed in these ways but is far deeper than that. It can communicate loudly, often without a word being spoken. For those who have known little real joy in their own lives it can be extremely attractive, causing them to question the source and covet it for themselves. More joy, more celebration, is needed in our lives. We can take it to those who have only known dullness and sadness, and their existence will be transformed. And as we begin to plumb the depths of knowing God for ourselves, joy will surprise us by being there.

Deepening relationship with God, coming to know Him more fully in heart and mind. Living out the reality of that knowledge in a climate of faith and drawing increasingly on His resources. It is this as a way of life that is the key to fleshing out His love for the world to see. Painstaking research and well laid plans will never be enough if we have not lives that are centred on God. It is only as we go deeper into Him that others will meet Jesus through us and broken lives will be changed.

EPILOGUE

Well, the time for lift off has finally come! The long months of preparation are over and what started as a dream is about to become a reality. Perhaps you are involved in something on your own or the scale of the project is not as large as those described here as examples? Or maybe the opposite is true, and the church is embarking on a course of action requiring a major input of resources? Whatever the circumstances, if you have implemented the recommended principles and have truly sought God, you can be confident that you are moving forward with Him into new depths in the life of faith.

Through positively expressing concern and reaching out to those in need the purposes of God will be fulfilled. You will be caught up in a way of life that has eternal consequences. Each small act clothed with the compassion of Christ will release something of His goodness into society. People's lives will be touched in unique ways by the love of God. Some will scarcely notice this while others will never be the same again.

Beginnings can be like a pebble thrown in a lake. The pebble itself disappears from view but the effects are seen in the ever widening ripples spreading out across the surface of the water. In the same way, it is impossible to tell at this stage what God will accomplish through your actions. One thing that you can be sure of is that the effects will be for good and not for harm.

Jean walked briskly into the interview room and sat down. She stated her reason for coming as being that she wanted information about retirement pensions as she was due to finish work as a district nurse in a few months time. She looked tired and strained but maintained a business-like veneer until the end of the conversation.

It was when the advice worker asked how she was feeling about the approaching life changes that the facade cracked. Quietly, interspersed with sobs, Jean talked about the recent death of her husband and the long lonely days that stretched out before her. Because of her training she knew the facts about bereavement but the knowledge did little to ease the pain of going through it. After a short while, she visibly gathered herself together, apologising for being foolish. She thanked the worker for her time and declined the offer of further contact. Despite this, and somewhat unusually, the worker felt strongly prompted to ask if she could pray for Jean before she left. Consent was given amidst more tears. The worker prayed briefly and then the conversation was concluded.

Jean didn't return and her name became just one of many amongst the referral forms in the filing cabinet. A small beginning in one person's life with seemingly little benefit. However, without the worker knowing it the effects were considerable in Jean's life. In that short interview something of the love of God had touched her, causing her to continue to seek comfort from Him through the pain of her loss. She began to pray and for the first time felt that somebody actually understood what she was going through. No more is known about her than that, but maybe the ripples from that one conversation are continuing to spread ever outwards in her life.

In contrast, Tony comes from a different generation and is completely unlike Jean. At nineteen, he was drifting through life with no job and no home. He had been thrown out of his parents' house because of his persistent drunkenness and petty theft. He lived on the fringes of society, living rough on the streets or when he could talk them into letting him, sleeping on friends' floors. When he had the money he dabbled with soft drugs. Generally his future looked quite bleak.

He had known little love in his nineteen years of life, with rejection being a more familiar experience. Consequently, he expected hostility from others and believed that no one could be trusted. People were there to be used, to get what you could out of them. Until one day a pebble dropped into his life in the form of an encounter with some Christians who were running a temporary shelter for homeless men on their church premises, just for the Christmas period.

Three years later, his life is transformed. He has a job, a steady girlfriend and shares a house with three other people. There are still occasions when he struggles with trusting people and his temper can be unpredictable. However, through consistent and persevering care on the part of a couple of those Christians he has been enabled to change. It certainly wasn't easy for those doing the caring. He gave them a rough time! But what he couldn't understand and what wouldn't go away was the love.

It was the love that ultimately melted the established defences to show the scared small child behind all the macho bravado. And so he eventually came to know for himself the God who lived in those Christians. One chance meeting, a pebble dropped into the lake of his life and he was never the same again.

What do these stories communicate? They remind us that all beginnings made with God have eternal significance. They say to us that true Christian social concern is taking God into the world that people might experience for themselves His goodness and love. And so, He is calling us to join Him in the adventure and cost of reaching out to embrace those in need.

Jesus said – "Peace be with you! As the Father has sent Me, I am sending you." (John 20:21).

NOTES

Chapter 1

1. *The Independent*, 23 September 1987.
2. *Roof*, Shelter (September 1987).
3. *Faith in the City – A Call for Action by Church and Nation: Report of the Archbishop of Canterbury's Commission on Urban Priority Areas* (Church House Publishing, 1985), 176ff.
4. Ibid.
5. *Church Growth and the Whole Gospel*, Peter Wagner (MARC Europe, 1987).
6. *Urban Christian*, Ray Bakke (MARC Europe, 1987).
7. Shorter Catechism.
8. *Joy in the New Testament*, William G. Morrice (Paternoster Press, 1984).

Chapter 2

1. The National Council for One Parent Families.
2. Age Concern, England.
3. *Social Trends*, (H.M.S.O., 1987).
4. Standing Conference on Drug Abuse (SCODA).

Chapter 3

1. "Men, Women and God" c/o London Institute for Contemporary Christianity, St. Peter's Church, Vere Street London, W.1.

Chapter 4

1. Quoted in *Issues Facing Christians Today*, John Stott (Marshall, Morgan and Scott, 1984).
2. Ibid.

APPENDIX I

Know Your Community

Where is the Community?

— What are the natural boundaries that mark the edge of the community? e.g. railway line, busy main road, canal, types of housing.
— Where are the officially laid-down boundaries? e.g. electoral ward or borough.
— Are there boundaries that are less clearly definable which are related to ethnic groupings?
— Where are the popular meeting places? Where can you find different types of people congregating together? e.g. Community Centre, popular pubs or clubs, sports centre, library, Bingo Hall.
— When is the community alive and full of people? When is it quiet? Are there particular places that are in use at these times?

Who are the Community?

— Distribution of different population groupings according to age, ethnic and social backgrounds?
— Are there any significant deviant minority groups? e.g. drug abusers.
— How much community consciousness is there? Do people identify with the area or see it as somewhere to move out of if possible?

— What degree of neighbourliness is there? Do people support each other in their local areas or is there a high proportion of isolated people? Are there any voluntary Good Neighbour schemes running?

— What is the population turnover rate? Do extended family members tend to live in the vicinity of each other?

What Type of Community Is It?

— What is the general atmosphere? Is it a place in which people feel safe?

— What is the environment like? Clean and well-kept or the opposite?

— Is there space for children to play safely? Are there parks and green spaces?

— What leisure activities are catered for in the area?

— What type of housing is there? Proportion of local authority to privately owned? Housing Association property?

— Is there any housing to meet special needs, and is there enough? e.g. bedsits for single homeless, sheltered accommodation for the elderly or disabled.

— Do people work in the community? What type of work is available?

— What proportion of residents are recently unemployed (last six months) or long-term unemployed (over a year)?

— What services exist for the community? How adequate are they? e.g. public transport, assistance in

times of crisis, medical provision, support services to help people in the home.
— What helping agencies, both voluntary and statutory are there? e.g. Social Services Dept., Citizens' Advice Bureau, Welfare Rights Group.
— What under-utilized physical resources are there? e.g. empty houses, shops; patches of derelict land; paper waste.

Community Perceptions?

— How do the local public generally see the Church? What do they think of your church?
— What would the public like to see your church doing in the community?
— What needs are there in the community that people are aware of and feel aren't being met? e.g. activities for different age groups, leisure facilities, employment prospects, helping agencies.

NOTE

Statistical information can usually be obtained from the Library Reference Department or Town Hall Information Section. Most likely sources include:
— 1981 Population Census (H.M.S.O.)
— Small Area Statistics
— Ward Profiles
— Local Authority departmental reports, e.g. Housing, Education, Social Services, Planning.

APPENDIX II

Community Survey Questionnaire
(Notes for Interviewers)

Aims

You may want to adapt this questionnaire so that it is more directly geared towards your local community or to identify more specific areas of need. In its present form, it has four aims in being of help to those who use it:

1. To gain a deeper understanding of the nature of the local community – strengths, weaknesses, neighbourliness, social centres, etc.

2. To gain a clearer understanding of individual and community "felt" needs rather than relying on assumptions.

3. To raise the general profile of your church and more specifically as a caring group of people who want their Christianity to be relevant and practical in its expression.

4. To prepare the way for a new project by raising people's awareness. It is not a questionnaire that is geared towards creating opportunities for personal evangelism but questions 14-16 will lend themselves to this if so desired.

Use

The questionnaire is best completed by means of personal interview rather than distributed through the post. You should introduce yourself by name and by church, politely requesting a few minutes of the respondent's time to help you with the survey. Explain that as a church you are concerned to find out what people think about the area and its needs, including their own personal needs. This is so that you can be actively involved, as a church, in serving the community and being a part of it in a way that makes a positive contribution.

Follow Up

If at all possible, it is important to follow up the questionnaire by making the results available to the community. This can be done in several ways e.g. distributing a circular letter around the neighbourhood, submitting the findings in the form of an article to the local newspaper and/or free press, or putting a poster up outside the church.

Then when it later comes to advertising the actual project you can refer back to the questionnaire. In so doing, you communicate the fact that you are prepared to listen to people and take what they think seriously.

COMMUNITY SURVEY

1. AGE   Under 21_____ 21-45_____ 46-65_____ Over 65_____

2. SEX_____

3. OCCUPATION_____

   UNEMPLOYED _____

4. DO YOU/YOUR PARTNER WORK LOCALLY?

   within 1 mile_____ 2-5 miles_____ further_____

5. HOW LONG HAVE YOU LIVED IN THIS AREA?

   under 1 year_____ 1-5 years_____ 6-10 years_____ longer____

6. HOW MANY PEOPLE DO YOU TALK TO IN A DAY
   FROM OUTSIDE THE HOME?

   (face to face)_____

7. WOULD YOU AND YOUR NEIGHBOURS VISIT
   ONE ANOTHER?

   several times a week_____occasionally_____rarely____never____

8. WHAT SORT OF NEIGHBOURHOOD IS THIS
   GENERALLY?

   friendly_____ unfriendly _____

9. WHAT DO YOU SEE AS THE MAIN PROBLEMS IN
   THE AREA?

10. WHAT FACILITIES DO YOU THINK ARE LACKING
    IN THIS AREA (a) (generally e.g. leisure, help with
    difficulties; (b) for different age groups e.g. elderly, young
    people, unemployed, women etc.)

11. WHO WOULD YOU LOOK TO FOR HELP IN A TIME
    OF CRISIS? (can tick more than one)

    Cope on your own if at all possible____Doctor____Church__

    A neighbour_____Family member_____Friend_____

    Other (specify)_____

12. WHERE WOULD YOU RECOMMEND SOMEONE TO
    GO LOCALLY IF THEY WANT TO

    (a) meet new people_____

    (b) have a good time_____

    (c) have advice about a personal problem_____

13. IF YOU HAD QUESTIONS ABOUT THINGS LIKE
    LIFE AFTER DEATH, THE MEANING OF YOUR
    LIFE, ETC., TO WHOM WOULD YOU TALK? (can tick
    more than one)

    Family_____Friend_____

    Someone that is "religous"_____Other (specify)_____

14. DO YOU ATTEND CHURCH?

    Regularly_____Rarely_____Never_____

15. WHAT WOULD YOU LIKE TO SEE THE CHURCH DO IN THIS AREA?

16. WHAT DO YOU THINK OF THE CHURCH TODAY GENERALLY?

Thank you very much for your help in completing this questionnaire

APPENDIX III

Caring Agencies

Statutory Agencies

All areas will have certain Statutory Agencies within them that have responsibility, exercised to varying degrees, for the welfare of the general public. Listed below are the main ones that you could usefully have contact with.

SOCIAL SERVICES DEPARTMENT (Area Office and the person centrally responsible for volunteers, voluntary organisations, Under fives etc.)

PROBATION DEPARTMENT

DEPARTMENT OF HEALTH AND SOCIAL SECURITY

HOUSING DEPARTMENT (Welfare Section and Homeless Persons Unit)

EDUCATION DEPARTMENT

DEPARTMENT OF EMPLOYMENT/JOB CENTRE/CAREERS SERVICE

POLICE (Community Beat/Liaison Officer)

G.P. PRACTICES/HEALTH CENTRES (Receptionists are often key people to talk to!)

Voluntary Agencies

(Voluntary does not necessarily mean unpaid for work done, but more that the agency concerned is not required by law to fulfil certain responsibilities.)

All areas will have a range of Voluntary Agencies geared towards meeting the needs of particular groups of the public. These vary greatly in size and scope of activities, with many being part of a larger national body e.g. Citizens' Advice Bureau, Samaritans. They are funded from a variety of sources including central and local government finance, and charitable giving.

Listed below are some of the main Voluntary Agencies that are likely to exist in your area:

VOLUNTARY SERVICE COUNCIL (Umbrella organisation to which most local voluntary Agencies will be affiliated in some way. May have a slightly different name in your area.)

CITIZENS' ADVICE BUREAU (General advice and information agency. Covers a wide range of concerns.)

SAMARITANS (Crisis support and counselling service. Mainly telephone contact.)

MARRIAGE GUIDANCE COUNCIL (Usually have long waiting lists.)

FAMILY CENTRES/WOMEN'S REFUGE, ETC (Provision of these varies greatly between areas.)

COMMUNITY CENTRE (Many areas have these as a focal point for social and community activities.)

VOLUNTEER ORGANISATIONS e.g. VOLUNTEER BUREAU (Act as clearing house for people who are willing to give time, free of charge, to members of the community who have particular needs e.g. elderly needing help with the garden.)

There are various other agencies such as Welfare Rights Groups, W.R.V.S., Age Concern, Pensioners' Rights, Law Centres, services for particular ethnic groups, and many others.

Agencies in Your Area

In order to find out what there is in your area you will obtain information from:

> THOMPSONS LOCAL DIRECTORY
> > (front pages)
> LOCAL LIBRARY
> > (useful sources of general information)
> INFORMATION DEPARTMENT IN
> > LOCAL TOWN HALL

and it is always useful to talk to the VOLUNTARY SERVICES COUNCIL, mentioned above. They may well have a directory of caring agencies working in your area.

APPENDIX IV

Project Ideas List

This "ideas list" is not exhaustive and there are probably many other suggestions that you could add to it. Some of these ideas encompass large-scale projects (requiring more finance, time, people-power and other resources), whilst others can be carried out by small groups of people or by individuals getting involved with existing agencies/groups (either secular or Christian).

IDEAS

Elderly

— Advice, information, help with filling in forms service. Pensioners' rights.
— Clubs and luncheon clubs.
— Recreational activities e.g. old-time dancing, keep-fit classes, drama.
— Retirement preparation classes and discussion groups.
— Legal advice e.g. wills etc.
— Coffee mornings.
— Set up volunteer scheme to help the elderly/housebound with practical tasks e.g. gardening, help with moving home.

— Good neighbour schemes/street warden schemes.

— Taking elderly people shopping.

— Sewing and knitting groups (provide old fashioned sewing machines!)

— Tea dancing for recently retired and active.

— Talks on nutrition, flower arranging, particular types of cookery, DIY, security in the home.

— Visiting isolated elderly people.

— Provision of Sheltered Housing in co-operation with a Housing Association and/or local authority.

— Verbal history project/Reminiscence group.

Children/Young People

— Playgroups, parent and toddler groups, nursery, "opportunity" groups (playgroup for disabled and able-bodied children).

— Involvement in local schools.

— Youth counselling service (within school or based at church).

— Youth Centre.

— Summer play schemes, holiday clubs.

— Set up an adventure playground.

— Local arts competition.

— Provide a place for fathers and mothers who have access to their children (after divorce) to bring them.

— "Latch-key" kids club.

— Teaching skills e.g. job applications, interviews etc.

— Toy Library (for use by able-bodied/disabled children).

— Opportunities for painting large murals (brighten up some of our churches on the outside).

— Pets' corner/city farm etc.

— Babysitting (broad age range) to support families under pressure etc.

— Christian education.

— Sports activities.

— Late night/all night coffee bar facility.

— Car/motor bike maintenance courses.

— Drama/music activities.

— Non alcoholic pub.

— Playbus (mobile playgroup/learning centre for under fives).

General

— Liaison with local Fire Station e.g. people badly affected by fire damage.

— Victim support scheme.

— Telephone counselling service (general or specialised).

— Advice Centre (specialising in one area e.g. housing or general approach).

— Teaching English to newcomers to Britain e.g. Bangladeshi community (mainly a need of women and older people).

— Sports and get-fit activities.

— Weight training for men.

— Art centred projects (general or for a special group e.g. disabled).

— Adult education.

— Training schemes and variety of projects with unemployed people.

— Centre for recreation, support and teaching of skills for the unemployed.

— Open a launderette & coffee facility for the local community.

— Support for those suffering with drug or alcohol related problems.

— Use of extended households to care for the lonely and needy.

— Support of recently discharged psychiatric patients.

— Support of families where one member needs a lot of care e.g. mentally handicapped child or adult, elderly confused spouse or parent.

— Self defence classes for women/disabled.

— Transcribing books into braille or onto tape for those with a visual handicap.

— Crisis Centre for those who have experienced rape, sexual abuse, domestic violence.

— Set up a Neighbourhood Watch Scheme (contact local police for information).

— Jesus Action Project (being available to help with any tasks in the community or refer onto those who can help e.g. decorating, changing a plug).

— Skills exchange (linking local skills offered with those in need).

— Community Shop e.g. second-hand children's clothes.

— Support for the mentally handicapped moving out of hospital into small self-supporting units in the local community.

— Involvement in local hospital e.g. long term psychiatric and mental handicap, children's wards.

— Involvement in community issues e.g. poor housing, helping set up a tenants association, need for pelican crossing.

— Special events tackling relevant areas e.g. a doctor talking on "Coping with Stress".

— Second hand clothing/furniture facility.

— Soup kitchen for alcoholics, homeless people, etc.

— Coffee and craft shop with literature.

— Set up an arbitration service (employer/employee; neighbour disputes etc).

— Bereavement support scheme.

— Arrange local festival/carnival or participate in existing one.

— Organise a street party.

— Support groups for single parents.

— Family life seminars/discussions.

— Task centred groups for isolated mums e.g. hairdressing, make-up, cookery.

— Marriage counselling.

— Clubs/groups with a special focus e.g. for stroke victims, mentally handicapped teenagers.

— Support groups for local child-minders, prospective adoptive parents, foster parents etc.

— Helping homeless people e.g. rights advice, good quality B & B facilities, Housing Associations.

— Helping unemployed people set up small businesses (e.g. painting and decorating, electrical) that will in turn serve the needs of the local community e.g. the elderly.

— Pregnancy testing and Counselling service.

— Support groups for AIDS sufferers/their families.

— Practical help in the home for AIDS sufferers.

Fount Paperbacks

Fount is one of the leading paperback publishers of religious books and below are some of its recent titles.

☐ THROUGH SEASONS OF THE HEART
                                    John Powell   £4.95
☐ WORDS OF LIFE FROM JOHN THE BELOVED
                                    Frances Hogan   £2.95
☐ MEISTER ECKHART Ursula Fleming   £2.95
☐ CHASING THE WILD GOOSE Ron Ferguson   £2.95
☐ A GOOD HARVEST Rita Snowden   £2.50
☐ UNFINISHED ENCOUNTER Bob Whyte   £5.95
☐ FIRST STEPS IN PRAYER Jean-Marie Lustiger   £2.95
☐ IF THIS IS TREASON Allan Boesak   £2.95
☐ RECLAIMING THE CHURCH Robin Greenwood   £2.95
☐ GOD WITHIN US John Wijngaards   £2.95
☐ GOD'S WORLD Trevor Huddleston   £2.95
☐ A CALL TO WITNESS Oliver McTernan   £2.95
☐ GOODNIGHT LORD Georgette Butcher   £2.95
☐ FOR GOD'S SAKE Donald Reeves   £3.50
☐ GROWING OLDER Una Kroll   £2.95
☐ THROUGH THE YEAR WITH FRANCIS OF ASSISI
                                    Murray Bodo   £2.95

All Fount Paperbacks are available at your bookshop or newsagent, or they can be ordered by post from Fount Paperbacks, Cash Sales Department, G.P.O. Box 29, Douglas, Isle of Man. Please send purchase price plus 22p per book, maximum postage £3. Customers outside the UK send purchase price, plus 22p per book. Cheque, postal order or money order. No currency.

NAME (Block letters) _____

ADDRESS_____

_____

_____

While every effort is made to keep prices low, it is sometimes necessary to increase them at short notice. Fount Paperbacks reserve the right to show new retail prices on covers which may differ from those previously advertised in the text or elsewhere.